Bertie Angammana was called to the Bar (Lincoln's Inn) in 1983 and is a practicing barrister. Prior to the onset of Covid-19 Pandemic in 2020, he has been managing diverse cases from the trial courts to the appeal courts. He was led by late Sir Desmond de Silva (QC) in many criminal trials, has been led by Mr Alper Riza QC (Part-Time Recorder) in civil and criminal trials, by Mr Martin Bowley QC in a murder trial, Late Mr John Platts-Mills QC in a drug trial and Late Mr Michael Driscoll QC in an insurance claim. He has prepared students for professional exams and has worked as a part-time lecturer in various schools and polytechnics in London. His Educational Credentials are LLB (Honours) London, PGCE (FE) University of Greenwich, LLM (LSE/SOAS), Attorney-at-Law (Sri Lanka).

This book is dedicated to the solicitors who instructed me during my career, senior members of the Bar who led me in various trials and to all my clients who instructed me to represent and conduct their cases.

Bertie Angammana

COMPLIANCE RULES FOR BARRISTERS

AUSTIN MACAULEY PUBLISHERS™

LONDON * CAMBRIDGE * NEW YORK * SHARJAH

A CIP catalogue record for this title is available from the British Library.

ISBN 9781398455030 (Paperback)
ISBN 9781398455047 (ePub e-book)

www.austinmacauley.com

First Published 2022
Austin Macauley Publishers Ltd®
1 Canada Square
Canary Wharf
London
E14 5AA

Resources used:

The Handbook of the Bar Standards Board

The Bar Council Guidance Notes

Data Protection Act 2018

Decided cases in relation to Data Protection.

The rules and regulations are changed from time to time depending on the evolving circumstances. Therefore, please update the documents accordingly. This book is primarily meant for the sole practitioners (sole practising barristers in England and Wales), but the information could be of help to those lawyers practising in common law jurisdictions because most commonwealth countries adapt the code of conduct and ethics based here in the UK subject to their local and domestic legislation.

Chapters pursuant to the Data Protection Act 2018 and certain sections of the Information Commissioner's Guidance may be of interest to other professionals such as pharmacist, dentists and doctors.

Chapter 1

Ten Core Duties of a Barrister are Set Out in the Handbook of the Bar Standard Board.

Core Duty 1: You must observe your duty to the court in the administration of justice.

Core Duty 2: You must act in the best interests of each client.

Core Duty 3: You must act with honesty and integrity.

Core Duty 4: You must maintain your independence.

Core Duty 5: You must not behave in a way which is likely to diminish the trust and confidence which the public places in you or in the profession.

Core Duty 6: You must keep the affairs of each client confidential.

Core Duty 7: You must provide a competent standard of work and service to each client.

Core Duty 8: You must not discriminate unlawfully against any person.

Core Duty 9: You must be open and co-operative with your regulators.

Core Duty 10: You must take reasonable steps to manage your practice, or carry out your role within your practice, competently and in such a way as to achieve compliance with your legal and regulatory obligations.

Please refer to the *Handbook of the Bar Standard Board* for further information.

Mandatory rules

Rule C159.4 and the Transparency Standards Guidance. Factors which might influence the timescales of a case and describe the nature of the legal services that you provide.

Rule C103.1 and the Transparency Standards Guidance. You must mention that you are "regulated by the Bar Standards Board" or "Authorised and Regulated by the Bar Standards Board".

Rule C101.2.a and the Transparency Standards Guidance. Set out in detail your complaints procedure and how to complain to the Legal Ombudsman and time limits for making a complaint.

Rule C101.2.b & c and the Transparency Standards Guidance. Set out link to the decision data page on the Legal Ombudsman website and/or the BSB Barristers' Register.

Additional Rules for Certain Direct Public Access Work

Paragraph 3 of the Bar Standards Board's Price Transparency Policy statement – The new Transparency Rules came in to force on 01 July 2019.

Rule C160 and the Transparency Standards Guidance. Please provide detailed information on costs and/or up to date costs.

Rule C166.2 and the Transparency Standards Guidance. Set out the circumstances in which fees may be varied in the process of the litigation.

Rule C166.3 and the Transparency Standards Guidance. State whether your fees include VAT.

Rule C166.4 and the Transparency Standards Guidance. Provide sufficient information in relation to additional costs such as disbursements, court fees for issuing Applications Issuing Fees, etc.

Rule C168 and the Transparency Standards Guidance. Set out the description of the relevant Public Access services (including a concise statement of the key stages and an indicative timescale for the key stages).

Chapter 2

Following passages are taken from the Bar Council Guidance Notes

Prohibition on Handling Client's Money

Client money and payments in advance Purpose: To address the interaction between the prohibition on handling client money and permissible payments in advance, Overview: Prohibition on handling client money – what is 'client money' – payments 'on account' of fees are not permissible – permissible up front, fixed fee arrangements – alternative of using third-party services Scope of application: Self-employed barristers issued by: The Ethics Committee First issued: June 2014 Last reviewed: July 2020 Status and effect: Please see the notice at end of this document. This is not "guidance" for the purposes of the BSB Handbook I6.4. The prohibition on self-employed barristers handling client money 1. Under the old (8th edition) of the Code of Conduct, self-employed barristers were prohibited from handling client money. 2. This prohibition remains in place under the new *Bar Standards Board (BSB) Handbook*. It has not been altered or watered down. 3. The prohibition is now in the following terms in rC73: "Except where you are acting in your capacity as a manager of an authorised (non BSB) body, you must not receive, control or handle client money apart from what the client pays you for your services." 2 4. This applies to public access cases just as much as to other cases. It also applies to barristers who obtain authorisation from the BSB to conduct litigation. The sole exception is the receipt of money in payment of fees. 5. Any breach of this prohibition amounts to professional misconduct and may be subject to enforcement or supervisory action by the BSB. What is client money? 6. Client money is defined in the Handbook as: a) money, securities or other assets beneficially owned by a client, or b) money, securities or other assets provided by, or for the benefit of, your client or intended by another party to be transmitted to your client. 7. So far as self-employed barristers are concerned, it excludes a fixed fee paid in advance, and a payment made in settlement of an accrued debt (i.e. the payment of fees or expenses which are already due to the barrister). Misconceptions about what this means in practice. 8. The prohibition is simple to state, but there may be some misconceptions about its practical application, particularly in relation to payments 'on account' of fees and other payments made in advance. BSB Guidance 9. The BSB has set out extensive guidance on the prohibition on handling client money at gC103 to gC112 in the Handbook, which repays reading in full. You should consider specifically the important points in relation to payments on account and other payments in advance. A practical starting point 10. One practical step to take in deciding whether you can accept a payment from a client might be to ask yourself this question: is it a payment of fees or expenses which are already due to me? 11. If it is, then it is likely to be permissible. If it is not, then it is likely to involve handling client money. 12. That test is too simplistic to cover all situations but may be a useful starting point. You will find a brief discussion below concerning where the dividing line may lie in cases involving fixed fee amounts payable in advance. 3 Payments on account 13. A payment on account does not represent fees which are already due: it represents money paid to a barrister, to be held 'on account' until fees fall due in the future. 14. Accordingly, one important effect of the prohibition is that you cannot accept a payment on account of fees. 15. The sole exception is where client monies are held by a third-party payment service which complies with rC74(see further below). Payments through chambers or others 16. The prohibition on accepting payments on account applies both to payments made to you and to payments made into or held in your chambers' bank account. 17. Monies held by chambers which do not represent fees which are already due to a member of chambers are just as much client monies as monies held by an individual barrister. 18. Accordingly, such monies held by your chambers which relate to you are likely to be held (or are likely to be regarded by the BSB as being held) on your behalf, putting you in breach of the prohibition on handling client money. Similarly, those barristers responsible for administering or controlling your chambers' bank account may also be in breach of the Handbook by permitting or participating in a breach of the prohibition by you. 19. The prohibition also applies to monies paid to or held by a 'ProcureCo', and through other arrangements which give you control over monies belonging to a client. 20. As stated in gC103-104: "The prohibition in Rule C73 applies to you and to anyone acting on your behalf, including any 'ProcureCo' being a company established as a vehicle to enable the provision of legal services but does not in itself supply or provide those legal services. Rule C73 prohibits you from holding client money or other client assets yourself, or thorough any agent, third party or nominee. Receiving, controlling or handling client money includes entering into any arrangement which gives you de facto control over the use and/or destination of funds provided by or for the benefit of your client or intended by another party to be transmitted to your client, whether or not those funds are beneficially owned by your client and whether or not held in an account of yours." 4 21. To put it simply, the prohibition on handling client monies cannot be avoided or side-stepped by using a chambers' bank account (or any other, similar arrangement) to receive or hold monies. Fixed fees in advance 22. If you agree to be paid a fixed fee for a piece of work, and that the fee will be payable before you start work, then you will be allowed to accept payment of that fee before any work is done. Such a payment is not client money, because it belongs to you as a payment of fees already due to you as soon as it is received. 23. If you subsequently come under an obligation to return the payment (for example, the fee was for a hearing which got cancelled) then you can do so without breaching the prohibition on handling client money. This is because the money would be treated as yours when received by you as a fee for work you had agreed to do. Therefore, you are not returning client money which you had been holding on account; you are making the payment out of your own money pursuant to an obligation you have to re-imburse the client. Other permitted arrangements 24. There are also two other types of arrangement which are allowed. 25. First, you and your client may agree that you will be paid a fixed minimum amount in advance, with the possibility of an additional fee falling due in defined circumstances (e.g. if the work reasonably takes longer than a specified number of hours). 26. An example might be as follows; Say that you charge an hourly rate of £100, and you anticipate that a piece of work will take ten hours. You, thus, estimate the resulting fee at £1,000. You and your client might agree that your client will pay you a fixed minimum fee of £1,000 before you do any work, but that if it reasonably takes you longer than ten hours, then your client will pay you for the additional time spent at your hourly rate. The resulting agreement is that you will be paid £1,000 in advance and will be entitled to keep that full amount even if the work takes you less than ten hours, but you will be entitled to an additional fee if it takes longer. 27. In order to be permissible, the terms of any such agreement will need to be clear, including as to how any additional fee will be calculated, (see rC22) and such an arrangement should only be made with a client who can reasonably be expected to understand its effect, and who appears to do so. 28. In connection with that first type of arrangement, you should pay attention to the first to third bullet points, and the last bullet point at gC107. This is quoted in the next paragraph. 5 29. The second type of arrangement is similar but involves an additional possibility that an amount may be payable back to your client. This is outlined at gC1071. The permissible 'pay back' element is explained at length in the fourth bullet point: "If you have decided in principle to take a particular case you may request an 'upfront' fixed fee from your prospective client before finally agreeing to work on their behalf. This should only be done having regard to the following principles: • You should take care to estimate accurately the likely time commitment and only take payment when you are satisfied that: - it is a reasonable payment for the work being done; and – in the case of public access work, that it is suitable for you to undertake. • If the amount of work required is unclear, you should consider staged payments rather than a fixed fee in advance. • You should never accept an upfront fee in advance of considering whether it is appropriate for you to take the case and considering whether you will be able to undertake the work within a reasonable timescale. • If the client can reasonably be expected to understand such an arrangement, you may agree that when the work has been done, you will pay the client any difference between that fixed fee and (if lower) the fee which has actually been earned based on the time spent, provided that it is clear that you will not hold the difference between the fixed fee and the fee which has been earned on trust for the client. That difference will not be client money if you can demonstrate that this was expressly agreed in writing, on clear terms understood by the client, and before payment of the fixed fee. You should also consider carefully whether such an arrangement is in the client's interest, taking into account the nature of the instructions, the client and whether the client fully understands the implications. Any abuse of an agreement to pay a fixed fee subject to reimbursement, the effect of which is that you receive more money than is reasonable for the case at the outset, will be considered to be holding client money and a breach of rC73. For this reason, you should take extreme care if contracting with a client in this way. • In any case, rC22 requires you to confirm in writing the acceptance of any instructions and the terms or basis on which you are acting, including the basis of charging." 30.

If all of those requirements are strictly complied with, and if the correct legal analysis is that you do not hold money belonging to your client at any point, then 1 This original gC107 was revised and expanded in the Second Edition of the Handbook, published in April 2015. Paragraph 28 quotes the revised and expanded guidance. 6 there will be no breach of rC73. However, as the guidance indicates, it will be far from easy to be confident that this outcome has actually been achieved, and it may be difficult for you to demonstrate both that your client understood the implications of such an arrangement (including what it meant in legal and practical terms for no part of the 'upfront' payment to be held on trust) and that this was in your client's interest. You might readily find that you have crossed the line and have handled client money. The Bar Council suggests that the BSB's guidance should be taken as containing a clear warning of the difficulties and risks involved in such an arrangement, and that you should take very great care indeed if you decide to pursue this possibility in any particular case. Third party payment services 31. The most straightforward way of achieving a result similar to that of requiring money to be paid on account is likely to be to use a third-party payment service (such as an escrow provider) which complies with rC74. 32. The availability of such services – and any decision not to use them – might be taken into account by the BSB if you were to breach rC73 by entering into an arrangement involving a prohibited payment on account, but that would be a matter for them. If you use an escrow or other third-party payment service you should ensure it complies with the guidance in gC108 to gC111. One of the key requirements is that the provider is not holding the money as your agent and that it cannot be paid out without the client's consent. Another is that the client's money will be safe and there is guidance on how you may satisfy yourself as to this in gC110. Further information 33. If you need further information or assistance on the prohibition on handling client money, then the Bar Council's Ethical Enquiries Service would be pleased to try to assist you (please email Ethics@BarCouncil.org.uk). *Important Notice*: This document has been prepared by the Bar Council to assist barristers on matters of professional conduct and ethics. It is not "guidance" for the purposes of the BSB Handbook I6.4, and neither the BSB nor a disciplinary tribunal nor the Legal Ombudsman is bound by any views or advice expressed in it. It does not comprise – and cannot be relied on as giving – legal advice. It has been prepared in good faith, but neither the Bar Council nor any of the individuals responsible for or involved in its preparation accept any responsibility or liability for anything done in reliance on it. For fuller information as to the status and effect of this document, please see here.

The above duties and rules are not the complete list. Therefore, please refer to the Handbook of the BSB for detailed information. Please contact the Bar Council Ethical Enquiries Service for advice and guidance of the Transparency Standards Guidance if you need further help and advice.

Bar Council issued information (five pages) in relation to Using a Third Party Payment (or Escrow) Service in August 2021. Please refer to Bar Standard Board Handbook prohibition on holding money rC73, gC106, gC107, gC103,. In relation to Third Party Providers – see rC73, rC74, gC109, gC110 and ,gC111. Please read the important notice on 5 of the information leaflet.

Chapter 3
Regulatory Return

Barristers in chambers with various clerks and administrators have facilities and technical support. Such help and support is not always available to sole practising barristers. Therefore, it is possible for the Bar Council to select a sole practising barrister to ensure that he or she has adequate safeguards for their respective clients. Therefore, the Bar Council would expect the member of the Bar to provide the Bar Council with the information requested to ensure that your practice is safe from the Clients' point of view and to make sure that you comply with all the professional requirements of the bar.

If, however, there are failing in your practice, with the compliance rules, etc., the Bar Council would advise and guide you to achieve the required standard to ensure that the clients are safe in your supply of the legal services.

A. You must have a Complaint handling procedure

Please see the **draft Client Care Letter and the Fact Sheet** which deals with details of the duties that a barrister must comply in his or her practice and when dealing with complaints. If you make a mistake in the procedure, please inform the client that he or she is entitled to obtain independent legal advice.

B. Lay clients do not have the additional protection of another legal professional involved in their case when he or she instructs a sole practitioner.

Therefore, please make sure that in your Client Care Letter that there will be another counsel taking over their cases if you are not available due to work or for any other commitments.

Always try to be in touch with other members of the Bar who do Direct Public Access work either from the established chambers in the city or other sole practitioners practising individually so there are no circumstances where the lay client would not have an additional protection if you are not available to conduct his case for whatever reason.

C. Please try to be in touch with established Chambers in the City. If there is a problem, then you will always have the support of the clerks in those chambers to arrange representation for your clients if you are not available for whatever reason.

D. Furthermore, if the case is complex, it is good practise to involve a senior member of the Bar after explaining the reason why the client needs two counsel.

E. Immigration, Crime, and Family Law (cases involving children) and vulnerable clients (those with mental health issues and old clients) – Please take additional precautions when you undertake instructions from such clients. Where possible, it is good practise to undertake instructions from such vulnerable clients via Solicitors firms. Therefore, make sure that you are known to several Solicitors firms dealing with such cases so that you could ask their help in case you have to refer a vulnerable client for them to take instructions and prepare the Brief for you so that the client has adequate safeguards.

Current Health Crisis

In the recent global pandemic, it is essential that all law practitioners (barristers, solicitors, para legal staff, pupil barristers and trainee solicitors) attend seminars online, and make sure their clerks, who assist them, attend those seminars. There are various different professional seminars conducted online by various academic institutions and professional organisations after the pandemic. Such online courses would also be considered as continuing professional development. I have not listed the names of various organisations providing seminars but I strongly advise the members of the respective profession to seek guidance in relation to the various organisations providing online seminar for professional development. Following seminars may be repeated online. Therefore, please keep a look out and register to attend the seminar online. The places may be limited. Therefore, please remember to book it online as soon as you see the seminar is advertised because there is a great demand for such free online seminars.

GDPR seminars organised by the Bar Council

Family legal aid billing

Criminal legal aid billing

Non-family – Civil Legal Aid billing

Remote Hearings

Financial Crime and Fraud

Family Law Seminar

Wills and Probate

Regulatory Equality

Data Recovery Seminar

Equality and Diversity Forum Eventbrite

Annual Bar and Young Bar Conference

EU Law after Brexit

Virtual Seminar

In addition to the above, I advise all those legal practitioners to attend various other seminars such as Zoom Virtual Webinars for the areas of their respective practice.

New Risks Due to the Pandemic

I have experienced the following problems and issues dealing with the courts.

i. Courts do not have staff to deal with the volume of paperwork especially when there is e-filing, and when sent the documents by either email (encrypted) or by CJSM.

ii. The result is when the cases are listed judge do not have all the papers. Once I was told there are almost 200 emails, that the court receive in a day but only one staff to deal with all those emails.

iii. It is impossible to speak to a member of the staff in a court almost most of the times. I, and my staff were told by a voice message that we are 91 on the line or 77 on the line and so on and in fairness to the pre-recorded voice messages we were also told that our calls were important and to hold on and we are moving up in the call que and continue to hold. Rather unexpectedly after a while, the phone line gets disconnected.

iv. Even emergency applications are not dealt with even though there is an emergency phone line for emergency applications. I have also experienced at the last moment the applications which were listed for hearings (including emergency applications for injunctions, non-molestation and occupation orders, etc.) are vacated without even informing the lawyers that the hearings were vacated (I have the contemporaneous notes, case references, case names and the courts where I have experienced these difficulties).

v. Cases are transferred from one court to another with not any updates as to what was happening.

vi. Directions are given without any consideration of the issues involved. I have information that this happens when the cases are listed before judges e.g. a part-time recorder is asked to deal with a family law case when perhaps she or he does not have any experience to deal with such cases simply because the court is unable to find a family court judge with relevant knowledge and experience to deal with the case at hand. It is common these days to see that judges, with a totally different experience, are sitting in family courts or in civil courts with no experience to deal with family issues – example; when a man (an old man suffering from cancer, mental health issues and all other ailments) was evicted from his house and changed the locks by his wife and his daughter without any evidence of violence or any other good reason, for convenience, the case was simply adjourned rather than hearing the case and to make the orders such as *"without any finding of any violence but the case was vacated and re-listed before a family court"*. It is within my experience that the next hearing would not come before a court for another six months or even for years in this pandemic. All that time the victim is out on the road exposed to Covid19 virus.

vii. I have cases such as motoring offences are adjourned almost every two months since March 2020 and misleading information was given to my clients that their respective case was listed for hearing but when they turned up in the court, the security staff informed us the case was vacated and offered an apology perhaps from the court after several days or weeks. I have no reason to doubt that other members of the legal profession, too, has experienced such novelties to the detriment of the litigants in this pandemic.

viii. If letters are dropped in the drop box in civil courts and in family courts, the letters and documents never get attended in time contrary to what the courts say that those letters and the documents in the drop box would be attended to the following day. Cheques enclosed with the paperwork do not get cleared on time and the clients suffer not issuing their applications or Claim forms as expected within the timeframe thus prejudicing their Claims.

New Opportunities

Remote hearings were not uncommon, I first undertook a remote hearing in 2010 in the Central London County Court. It was a road traffic accident in which my client (young accountant with a family) suffered terrible injury and had to walk with walking aids for the rest of his life. He came here as a skilled worker to work in a computer company after his visas were expired, he went back to his native country.

He gave evidence remotely via video link. Certain courts even in those days had been equipped with such technical facilities to conduct such trials and conference hearings remotely. Similarly, various immigration courts in London and surrounding areas had similar facilities to conduct hearings via video links available for some years. Such hearings are quite common since the pandemic.

Those days, the barristers and solicitors had to attend the court to conduct such hearings, but since the pandemic, such hearings are conducted over the phone if it only involves minor issues and directions, etc. and on Zoom on the computer or laptop of the barrister or counsel sitting at home. It is quite common for the parties also to take part in the trial on Zoom either from their computer or from their mobile. Of course, formalities are there that the parties take the oath before giving evidence and the room where the parties give evidence should be safe and without anyone attending the hearing except the parties and their lawyers and the judge and the clerk of the court. Such hearing now takes place even in case such as abduction cases where the parties and their children in different jurisdiction e.g. perhaps in Pakistan, India, Malaysia and Singapore, etc.

i.   Remote hearing are now taking place almost in most cases except Jury Trials and in some magistrates' court cases.

ii.   I advise all those who engage in legal profession to get used to the remote hearings either over the phone, Zoom, Webinar, and Skype.

iii. Remote hearings save time travelling to a court just to make an application for an adjournment, etc.

iv.   Furthermore, cases are effectively dealt with even though they are dealt remotely because paperwork such as submissions and skeleton arguments are submitted to the court in advance. But the problem is there are times that all the documents are not placed before the judge. There are such technical difficulties due to the shortage of staff working in the courts or staff without sufficient experience.

v.   It is at times difficult to point to case law, page numbers effectively in remote hearings. If a lawyer is before the judge, he or she could easily ask him or her to read the most relevant submissions rather than inviting him to look into papers from a distance. Perhaps the judge may also be working from home with distractions of noise, etc. which is not uncommon when working remotely due to interference with satellite signals as well as other common disturbances such as children and from traffic nearby depending on the location where the parties are dealing with the case on Zoom.

It is prudent for the legal practitioners to make relevant modifications considering the above novel problems and the new working order to serve the clients and to assist the courts.

Legal Practitioners need to have their office rooms well organised, without any distractions when remote hearings take place. It is good practice to have a member of the staff in the loop (either Zoom or on phone) so that he or she could take down notes. Please note that you should ask permission from the judge before you permit your staff to take part in the proceedings. Most judges may allow such practice and give you permission but there may well be judges who may not give such permission. Please bear in mind that you are not allowed to tape-record court proceedings, but you are as always allowed to take down notes. Please bear in mind to inform the judge and other party before you have any of your staff/clerks/pupils/trainees in the loop. There may be occasions that the opposite party may object to having anyone in the loop except the counsel/solicitor. On such occasions, do the best you can to take down notes contemporaneously.

Please make sure that you have passwords for your laptop, mobile phone, and for your briefcase.

i.   Make sure that your mobile phone company could delete the data in your mobile phone remotely if you lose your mobile phone.
ii.   Furthermore, ask them to install technical procedures to locate your mobile phone or laptop if it is inadvertently lost or stolen.

Youth Courts

Even if you have previous experience dealing with youth courts, I suggest that you undertake seminars and training before you undertake youth court cases involving juvenile defendants and children.

Money Laundering Regulations

It is good practice to attend seminars dealing with financial fraud even if you do not undertake such cases so that you would be in an experienced position to find out where your client finds his money to fund his litigation in certain circumstances where the fees are relatively high. Some years ago, Bar Council offered the facility of an Escrow Accounts with the Bar Council for clients when they expected to receive funds from their commercial dealings. The Bar Council has discontinued Escrow Accounts. There are new alternative methods of dealing with such cases, like opening a Third-Party Account. I advise those who are dealing with such financial transactions to undergo the relevant training before undertaking such work involving money laundering regulations. However, you must always conduct due diligence test on your clients before accepting instructions and your fees to ensure that you do not receive fees derived from money laundering activities either in the UK or from any other country.

1. Governance arrangements

i.   All you and your staff should endeavour to attend regular seminars. It is important that you continue to attend professional development training in the areas of your practice.

ii. If you practise from home, you must have an office room with access to your professional books, study material, computer, and facilities for remote working. You should also have access to libraries, and it is better to be a member of Legal Libraries such as the Institute of Advanced Legal Studies. It is also good practice to have arrangements with Lincoln's Inn, Middle Temple, Inner Temple, and the Inner Temple Library (conference rooms) to see your clients and to accommodate clients with disabilities such as wheelchair access. Such facilities were available previously, but I believe such facilities are no longer available in those libraries due to the pandemic.

iii. You should ensure that you could arrange conference rooms either in the city or in other areas where this is necessary to conduct conferences. If necessary, have your support staff assist if you have to deal with a client who has a physical disability such as wheelchair-bound clients.

2. Risk management

Proper arrangements must be made for ensuring confidentiality of clients' affairs.

You must take reasonable steps to ensure that your practice is efficiently and properly administered. It is mandatory to keep affairs of each client confidential.

i.   You must have passwords for your laptop, mobile phone and for your briefcase.

ii. Please endeavour to arrange with your mobile phone company to delete the data in your mobile phone remotely if you lose your mobile phone and to help you to locate the mobile phone if it is inadvertently lost or stolen.

iii. You must also **advise your staff to take measures so that they, too, would adhere to the above guidelines.**

iv. **Please do not take instructions from clients if they are with any other persons unless they give consent and that you think it is necessary for your client to be supported by a third party.**

v.   **Make sure that you have different folders for individual clients and their data do not get mixed up with other clients.**

vi. **You should advise your staff that they should not talk about individual client's affairs with anybody else.**

vii. **If you foresee a client has a potential conflict with any other client, you should inform them in advance and advise them to be separately represented due to a possible conflict of interest in the future.**

viii. Please ensure that your staff and you attend regular seminars to update our knowledge and experience.

3. Data Protection Act 2018

i.   It is good practice to have a shredder in your office to destroy unwanted documents.

ii. You could also engage a document destroying company when necessary.

iii. It is good practice to inform the client in writing before you destroy documents. You must make sure that the original documents are returned to the respective clients after either the conclusion of the case and/or after appeal.

iv. It is good practice in my view to keep copies of the court orders and inform the clients that you keep the copy of court orders and consent orders, etc. Please also advise them to keep their documents in a safe and secure place.

v. It is better to have a safekeeping box in the bank, so that you could keep important documents in the security safe.

vi. It is good practice to have waterproof boxes to keep case files.

vii. It is important that you attend Date Protection Seminars conducted by the Bar Council, and by Briefed GDRP Academy approved by the Bar Council. If you pass their examination, they will offer you GDPR Certification for barristers valid for a year.

You could also arrange the GDRP Seminars for your staff.

It is, in my view, essential to incorporate the following documents pursuant to the guidelines of the GDPR Seminars in your practice.

i. Data Processed Register and templates.
ii. Data Retention and disposal policy.
iii. Data Security Policy
iv. Mobile Working Policy
v. Privacy Policy

4. New Risks arising from the impact of the Pandemic

a. There are new risks especially in relation to drawing up wills, etc. Example: if a client is old and feeble and he wants to give instructions, you must make sure that he or she has the mental capacity to give you instructions. If the client was known to you before, you might know where or not the client has the capacity. In such situations, in addition to the due diligence tests as to his identity, etc., you must ask him to obtain a letter from his GP or any other healthcare professional that he has the capacity to give you instructions. In addition to the above, the issues as to his witnesses need to be considered. Due to Covid pandemic, they may be reluctant to travel outside. In an emergency situation, they may have to have a video link so that you would ensure the identities of the witnesses and when and where they sign.

b. **You must ensure that your staff understand their obligations**

i. Arrange training for your staff to attend not just Data Protection Legislation but also other seminars in the areas of your practice.
ii. Talk to them and explain the new developments in the areas of your practice.

c. **Arrangements with Third Parties** – It is good practice to engage the services of legal stationers for your photocopying, making trail bundles, etc. Their services may include printing, arranging document bundles, scanning and photocopying, all subject to confidentiality clause in their agreement.

When dealing with courts and other legal professionals – It is best practice to create CJSM account in addition to your Chambers email to communicate with courts and to exchange of information is safe and secure.

d. **Appropriate technical and practice security measure to avoid data breaches** i. I have antivirus protection in my computer in addition to my password. My staff, too, have similar devises.

5. Data Breaches that you have reported to the Information Commissioner's Office

If you identify any data breaches or any near misses, it is your duty to make a report.

Rule C65 – If you are subject to any disciplinary or other regulatory or enforcement by another regulator, you are under a duty to make a report.

6. Instances of Fraud, Regulatory or Near Misses

If you or your staff have suffered any losses due to fraud, suspected fraud, cyber-attacks, or other irregularity, you must report such incidents to the appropriate authorities. Your practice may experience some occasional difficulties in getting into the internet due to loss of signals or maintenance work in your area. But these are temporary issues and may not affect your ability to perform your work.

Please be aware about cyber-attacks which could maliciously disable computers, steal data, or use a breached computer as a launch point for other attacks. Therefore, ensure that your laptops has proper protections from such cyber-attacks. It is good practice to install an antivirus protection in your computer and update it often. You must advise your staff to install such antivirus protection in their computers. I have advised my staff to install such devise in their computers.

7. If you are currently using or that you are planning to introduce, new and innovative technology? You must be familiar with the relevant expertise and should inform the Bar Council

i.   Do you use technological equipment such as iPhones and other devices or tools that allows effective communication among your team?
ii.   Do you have facilities such as voice recognition available on your computer or phone?

If you are using such innovative technology, you must know their advantages, disadvantages and technical issues arising from such innovative technology.

iii. Covid19 pandemic led us to use technologies such as Zoom and Webinars where we conduct cases, conferences, and seminars with people from all around the globe.

Telephone operator provides telephone line service which is encrypted so that all those in the loop could be involve in the cases, directions, and trials.

However, one cannot from here be so sure about the privacy of the other participants if they are abroad.

Please state if you have identified any risks in such technology.

i. I personally do not think it is within your control to ensure how participants take part in the court proceedings from abroad. They do not come within the Rules and Regulations here and perhaps not subject to the guidelines of the professional organisation here in the UK. It is a matter for the organisers to ensure the privacy and confidentiality of the participants.

ii. I am aware that in some countries there are specially approved studios available for witnesses to give evidence from abroad. I conducted such a trial in the Central London County Court in 2010. During that period even in England only a limited number of courts were available for such hearings with a screen and a video link. Gradually this facility was extended to immigration trials, etc. However, the technology in this area is now well-developed and is a necessity.

iii. When such hearings are conducted remotely, there are interruptions such as dogs barking, children talking, and noises emanating either from vehicles or other disturbances perhaps due to poor satellite signals. There are occasions that the seminar needs to be re-scheduled due to problems associated with technology.

iv. Have you considered using such technology? As I have described, I use technology in this area within limits and I did not encounter serious issues or problems dealing with cases remotely. I personally do not intend to use any advance technological innovations. If it is a mandatory requirement from the Bar, then I am willing to undergo the necessary training to introduce such technology. I trust the reader of this guide would have a similar opinion.

v. If you have any suggestions as to how the BSB could enable us to make a greater use of technology or innovation, please state and make suggestions.

In my opinion, if such seminars are conducted by the Bar Council, they should be made available free to all members of the pupil barristers because there has been a sharp drop in fees for all the practitioners.

8. Summarise other key risks that you have identified and describe how you manage and control such risks.

i.   Financial and the ability to win enough good quality work to make your practice viable – Fee income for all the partitioners is dramatically reduced due to the pandemic. Most clients have lost their jobs and are no longer able to pay legal fees. But as lawyers, you have a moral and a professional obligation to continue with their cases. Therefore, instead of abandoning your client's cases, consider if you continue to work on their cases on a different basis (lower rate of fees or even on pro bono basis to deserving clients) and represent them remotely.

Most clients do not want to issue proceedings even online because there are court fees involved, vast majority of the clients, and cases are not exempt from paying the court fees to issue the proceedings. Most cases do not qualify for public funding.

ii. Market Risks – Encourage all your staff to attend online seminars and learn how to conduct cases remotely. Even though some barristers are willing to continue with the cases, there are practical difficulties.

iii. There are financial risks due to the pandemic. In case there is a need, one can approach the Bar Benevolent Fund.

iv. Reputation – All barristers are concerned with their reputation, therefore learn new technologies and adapt yourself to the new market conditions and new work ethics so that you would not lose your established reputation as a barrister.

v.   Health and well-being – Encourage all your staff to undertake some form of exercise every day and to go for a drive but ensure to comply with the guidelines by the government. Ask them to take exercises, remain focused and optimistic. Always support your staff if they have serious financial difficulties because they have been working with you and have given their services loyally to your clients. If you are unable to support them financially any longer, refer them to the proper authorities for help.

9. Do you foresee any other changes in external factors over the next 12 months?

i.   If the pandemic continues and intermittent lockdown takes place, undoubtedly there will be disruptions even to conduct cases remotely either by Zoom or by phone.

ii. Clients, who lost their jobs and livelihood, would not be in a position even within one year to secure employment. Even if they secure employment, they may not be able to finance litigation because they may well have incurred priority debts and liabilities rather than spending money on their ongoing or prospective litigation.

iii. If you or your chambers have pupils, they may well be affected because they may not be able to gain any practical experience in real court settings. Remote hearings are not the best way to get practical experience with clients, other members of the profession and court staff.

iv. Barristers are not an exception to escape from the hardships caused by the pandemic. They may also not be able to have any hope of securing livelihood. It may well be the case that they may have to look for alternative employment. What then is the prospective alternative employment, perhaps none either here in the UK or elsewhere in the world due to the pandemic.

v.   Speaking for myself, I have secured contracts with publishers to write books and some of them are already published.

vi. It, undoubtedly, will have a psychological impact on the members of the Bar, all other professionals as well as others (professionals or not) who lost their employment and could no longer secure any employment because there are no longer any jobs available except perhaps in the case of delivery companies and online service industry.

vii. The above are risks and are well within our common knowledge.

viii. There are several vaccines now available in this country as well in the world, therefore, there is hope in the long term after mass vaccination and herd immunity but the phobia of becoming sick would be in the mind of the public. So, there may well be the case for the scientists to develop an effective cure as well. All these issues would have an impact on the psychology of all of us, exposing some of us into anxiety, depression and so on.

10. Are you planning any other significant changes to your practice within the next 12 months?

i. I suggest that all members of the profession (solicitors as well as barristers), students and the staff to enrol with more seminars of their respective professional areas and learn new skills to deal with cases remotely or otherwise and to cope with the situations as they develop.

ii. I suggest there is a moral and professional duty to continue to represent the existing clients whether they could not afford to pay due to loss of their livelihood and employment.

iii. If there are suggestions to introduce advanced methods of conducting cases remotely, you and your staff should be very eager to participate and learn new technology as approved by the professional organisations.

iv. I do not anticipate that one could expand, set up an entity to accept pupils because there is no prospect of any new cases or reasonable income from the practice at present. This climate may change at some time in the future. Then, the chambers will have to reassess the situation to expand and develop the practice as a sole practitioner.

11. What are the financial projections for the year ending 31 March?

i. **Percentage change of income** – In my experience, it is anticipated there may be approximately in the region of 50% to 75% drop or even more. It is difficult to say this for certain for all partitioners because individual practitioner's source of their fee income is varied depending on the nature of practice and areas of practice. It is difficult to predict how much they would receive from their lay clients as well as from their professional (solicitors) for the year ending 31 March. If the clients are unable to pay, there is no point trying to persuade them to pay because they have good reasons and inability to raise funds for litigation. I heard stories that a very few members of the legal profession have not been affected financially as a direct consequence of the pandemic but, in my view, a large majority of the members experienced reduction in cases and consequential reduction in the fee income. Percentage income would be reduced even further if the restrictions due to the pandemic continue and the courts (civil, family and magistrates as well as vast majority of crown courts) remain closed for longer period.

ii. **Projected change in working hours** – Difficult to say exactly but one may estimate 65% reduced working hours depending on individual practitioner's workload. The new trend is that the practitioners and their staff spend time attending virtual seminars (some of the seminars are paid, and others are free online seminars with varying CPD points). It is obvious due to remote hearing as well due to closure of many court buildings (except for a limited number of jury trials, some criminal trials in magistrates courts, a small number of civil and family cases and injunctions) due to the pandemic, members of the Bar, solicitors and judges no longer spend time on travelling and waiting in the courts until cases are called. However, there are exceptions in some family courts and civil courts, the judges continue to attend the courts.

iii. Should the members of the Bar renew their practising certificates for the year? In my opinion, all members of the Bar should renew their practising certificates and remain optimistic and not take a negative view of the future unless they want to retire from the practice or for some other personal reason.

12. What other information would you like the BSB to be aware of in considering risks associated with our respective practices?

I have identified the risks as set out above. I advise other professionals to identify other risks factors if they have experienced due to the Covid19.

Client Service and Delivery

13. Are we compliant with the price, service and redress transparency rules?

This is a matter for individual practitioners to deal with making references to the requirements of the specific rules.

14. What changes have you made in response to the new transparency rules and what (if any) impact you observed since these changes have been introduced?

Regarding the aforesaid requirements

i.   Please check your Draft Client Care Letter and the Fact Sheet and amend those documents to comply with the recent Transparency Rules which came into force in July 2019.

ii.   If you are not sure, seek guidance and advice from the Bar Standard Board and Ethics if your Client Care Letter and the Fact Sheet comply fully with the requirements, and amend it where necessary.

iii.   Make sure that there are no barriers either to implement or to comply with the rules.

iv.   Please refer to the information and guidance when necessary to draft your **Client Care Letter and the Fact Sheet** to comply with the rules and guidance notes.

v.   If you notice any positive impact or any negative impact, make a note of it where necessary.

vi.   If you notice any change of behaviour of the clients because of the changes, make a record of it.

15. If you have clients that engage you with in a retainer arrangement, make a record of it.

16. How do you ensure that lay clients who want to complain feel able to complain, know how to complain and feel confident that their complain will be taken seriously?

i. The information on how to complain must be dealt with in your Client Care Letter.
ii. It is good practice to set out the Complaints Procedure in the Fact Sheet attached to your Client Care Letter.
iii. It is good practice and reassuring to the clients if you ask them personally if there are any issues that he or she wants to raise with you from time to time and ask them if they are happy with your services.
iv. It is good practice to ask your clients to complete a survey at the end of the case so that he or she could confidently say what they are unhappy about. This would assist you to improve your practice.
v. If you have received any complaints over the last 12 months, make a note of it in detail.
vi. Always give your clients the opportunity to talk to you or to your designated staff if they are unhappy with your chambers' services.
vii. If you have not identified themes from the clients' feedback, ensure that you amend your practice so that you will not repeat any mistakes.

17. Software that you use to manage your cases

i. Most practitioners use Microsoft Office 365 (Word, Excel, PowerPoint, Access, etc.)
ii. Make sure that you have Norton Antivirus protection and updates. Check your laptop or computer often to check that the new software is installed. Norton Antivirus protects risks such as cyber-attacks, trying to obtain data from your computer.
iii. Also communicate with courts and other professional via CJSM. Therefore, communications are protected. You can use your chambers' email, but the information must be protected and should carry the standard warning.
iv. Make sure that you have a calendar, diary, computer, mobile phone to record the dates that you should comply with directions, etc. thus

ensuring that you never have any problems remembering when you should comply with the directions. Furthermore, your staff must also keep a tab when you should comply with directions and attend hearing.

If you receive instructions from other sources (apart from solicitors, licensed access instructions and public access instructions received directly from clients), you must make a record of such instructions and the sources of such instructions and make statement to that effect in your Regulatory Return.

Practice Management

18. How do you ensure, where applicable, the staff working with you are competent to do so?

i.   Arrange seminars in the areas of your practice. Advise and ask your staff to get used to the remote hearings either over the phone, Zoom or Webinar and Skype.

ii.   Talk to your staff and find out if they are familiar with the areas of your practice even though some of them have been with you for some time. If they are new staff, ask for their CV, CRB checks if necessary and references.

iii.   If you identify any issues in relation to competence of your staff, help them to attend relevant seminars, advise and encourage them to read study material where appropriate.

19. If your pupils or staff raise any grievance, make a record of their complaints or grievance and assist them and reassure them.

20. Does your practice have an up-to-date Disaster Recovery Business Continuity Plan?

Major incidents including power failures, major cyber-attacks, and terrorist attacks

i.   Save your documents in an external hard drive.

ii. Make sure that you have a reputable and reliable antivirus protection in your computer.

iii. It is good practice to store documents in waterproof boxes in case of a flood damage.

iv. It is good practice to have a security box in the bank to store more important documents.

v.   Make sure that your property is protected by CCTV monitoring all around the property and you have an IP address so that you could frequently check your property from a distance.

vi. Make sure that you have a professional key holding company to hold keys to your property in case of an emergency and that you are not available. Example; CMS Key holding.

vii. Install an alarm system connected to CMS key holding, Group 4, Police, Fire and Ambulance.

viii. Always advise your clients that they should also keep copies of their documents in safe and secure place.

ix. Remember that it is always possible to obtain the copy of pleadings and documents from the opposite side subject to payment of photocopying and administrative charges.

x.   It is always possible to obtain copy of documents from the courts subject to the payments of photocopying and administrative charges.

xi. In certain situations, and circumstances, if the case is very old and the solicitors who instructed you are no longer in practice, you could always approach the Solicitors Archives and obtain the document (if they are still available) subject to a payment of their photocopying and administrative charges.

xii. It is advisable that you attend a seminar on Document Disaster Recovery. They will teach you how to save the documents in the Cloud. Check and see if your technical support company (e.g. PC world) would assist you to recover the data from your computer in case they are lost due to major unexpected disaster.

xiii.   If the intervention is necessary and the BSB needs to access your computer remotely, you should be able to allow access subject to GDPR Rules.

xiv.   Make arrangements in advance with other sole practitioners, other established chambers either in Central London or elsewhere and also with solicitors known to you in the event your practice is intervened or disrupted due to any other reason to take over your cases.

xv.   Do not hold any files that you should return to solicitors or clients.

21. As a Sole Practitioner, there are risks to your clients if you suddenly become unavailable and are unable to continue to provide your services.

i. Situations and circumstances, during which you are unable to provide services, must be set out in your Client Care Letter and alternative arrangements in such circumstances.

ii. It is good practice to develop contact with other chambers, and speak to the clerks of those chambers so that in a situation that you cannot continue with your services, those clerks may be able to and arrange representations for your clients if you are not available.

iii. You should also be in touch with other sole practitioners and solicitors as well, so that you could ask them to arrange representations for your clients if necessary.

The Covid19 Health Crisis and Risks

i.   Sickness of members of the Bar or any other professional is nothing new. You must always have an alternative plan to deal with your clients' cases if you are unwell, on holiday, or unavailable due to any other work commitment or for any other reason. This eventuality must be set out in your Client Care Letters. However, the scale of the problem is now much bigger due to the Covid19 global pandemic.

ii.   You have to adjust your practice to deal with cases in the areas of your practice to the best of your ability.

iii. You test your plan since the first lockdown was introduced, learn lessons from it and improve your experience to manage your practice well so as to avoid any problems.

iv. Make sure that your clients have the copy of the documents. Courts and other members of the bar could access documents via CJSM system in case they need to see the documents provided that they have appropriate authority from the clients and the courts to access the documents in the event that you have fallen ill.

v. Make sure that you have technical support plan with your service providers (e.g. PC World) so that they could retrieve lost data for whatever reason.

22. How do you monitor the changes in the BSB Handbook and make sure that you are up to date with regulatory requirements?

Read the new version when it is issued. Learn the changes and amendments made and do your best to comply with the regulatory requirements and attend seminars where necessary. If you have issues, contact the BSB and they will help you to resolve the issues.

23. What feedback do you have on the Code of Conduct in the BSB Handbook?

i. The way we practice in law as well as in all other professions is changed dramatically due to the pandemic not just here in the UK but all over the world.

ii. Remote hearings are helpful but there is a problem with the administration of remote hearings in courts and tribunals perhaps because they do not have staff to deal with the cases and telephone calls and correspondences with the courts.

iii. If time limits are applicable, it may be the case clients will have to apply for extension. Examples: to lodge an appeal or to comply with directions, or to issue proceedings within time limits set out by statutes.

Areas of Practice

24. The key controls that are in place for Public Access Instructions.

Training and Experience

Make sure that you undertake the training and keep attending seminars to update new areas of rules and regulations. Also ensure that your staff is familiar with the updates.

You must be familiar with the procedure that you have for assessing the suitability of a client for public access work.

Examples:

i.   If the case involves gathering information to draft witness statements, it may be the case that you would advise your client to instruct a solicitor or if they wish they could instruct you through a solicitor. This is to avoid any conflict of examination-in-chief, cross-examination, or re-examination in the event of a trial of the case.

ii. If you have represented another client involved in the case previously, avoid taking instructions from the new client because there may well be a conflict of interest between the parties involved.

iii. If they are entitled to legal aid (public funding), inform that they have the right to instruct a solicitor with legal aid franchise because you may not have the legal aid franchise. Then it is a matter for the solicitors to extend the legal aid to cover your services and fees.

iv. If the client is impecunious and he or she could not afford to pay your fees, advise them to seek representation from the Bar Pro Bono Unit. Historically this service was provided by the Bar Free Representation Unit. You could also advise them to seek other charitable organisations to represent their interest if they could not pay your fees.

v.   Always make sure that you conduct Due Diligence Test to ensure their identity (Passport or Photocard Driving Licence) and address (two utility bills in her or her name).

vi. If you are instructed by more than one client for the same case, take instructions from them individually to assess if there is a potential conflict of interest which would eventually turn out to be an actual conflict of interest and advise them to seek separate representation if you foresee any such problem. There are numerous situations and circumstances in Criminal as well as Civil Litigation that there are conflicts of interests between the clients.

vii. Make sure that the clients have the mental capacity to give you instructions if they were not known to you before and that they are old or if they have a history of mental illness. If you are not sure, ask them to obtain a report either from their GP or from their psychiatrist.

viii. Make sure that you own a calendar, diary, computer, mobile phone to record the dates that your client should comply with directions, etc. Also ask your staff to keep a tab when your client should comply with directions and attend hearings. Program your laptop/computer to record the time contemporaneously when you do your written work in addition to your notes in the counsel's notebook.

Information provided to the lay client

Information must be well set out in your Client Care Letter and the Attached Fact Sheet. If they are unable to understand English, you must arrange an interpreter to translate the information in the Client Care Letter and the Fact Sheet into their native language and get a statement signed by the interpreter and the client to that effect.

Record keeping

This must be clearly set out in your Client Care Letter and in the Fact Sheet.

25. What systems do you have in place to enable you to conduct litigation?

i. You should enrol for seminars for training to undertake litigation, and to correspond with third parties.

ii. Ensure that you have CJSM email system to communicate with the courts and other professional dealing with the case.

iii.   Also attend seminars to learn the e-filing system to upload the documents when necessary.

iv.   Update your diary when necessary and contemporaneously.

v.   Due to the pandemic, courts do not accept documents in the drop box placed in front of courts. Staff may advise you to send the documents by email. Therefore, please make sure that you have alternative methods to file and serve the documents in courts.

vi.   There are helpful seminars conducted by HMCTS and various other professional organisations to update your knowledge in the developing systems of communication and administrative procedures.

26. **If you undertake or supervise claims management activities in relation to the following areas of law, inform nature of such activities in the Regulatory Return.**

a)   Personal Injuries

b)   Financial products and services

c)   Housing disrepair

d)   Industrial injuries benefits

e)   Criminal injuries

f)   Employment

27. **Also set it out in the Regulatory Return inform if you undertake work that falls withing the scope of Money Laundering Regulations**

Barristers in Chambers with various clerks and administrators have the facilities and technical support. Such help and support is not always available to sole practising barristers. Therefore, it is possible for the Bar Council to select a sole practising barrister to ensure that he or she has adequate safeguards for their respective clients. Therefore, the Bar Council would expect the member of the Bar to provide the Bar Council with the information requested to ensure that your practice is safe from the clients' point of view and to make sure that you comply with all the professional requirements of the Bar.

If however, there are failing in your practice, with the compliance rules, etc., the Bar Council would advise and guide you to achieve the required standard to ensure that the clients are safe in your supply of the legal services.

A. You must have a Complaint Handling Procedure

Please see the **draft Client Care Letter and the Fact Sheet** which deals with details of the duties that a barrister must comply in his or her practice and when dealing with complaints. If you make a mistake in the procedure, please inform the client that he or she is entitled to obtain independent legal advice.

B. Lay clients do not have the additional protection of another legal professional involved in their case when he or she instructs a sole practitioner.

Therefore, please make sure that in your Client Care Letter that there will be another counsel taking over their cases if you are not available due to work or for any other commitments.

Always try to be in touch with other members of the Bar who does Direct Public Access work either from the established chambers in the city or other sole practitioners practising individually so there are no circumstances where the lay client would not have an additional protection in the event that you are not available to conduct his case for whatever reason.

Please try to be in touch with established Chambers in the City. If there is a problem, then you will always have the support of the clerks in those chambers to arrange representation for your clients if you are not available for whatever reason.

Furthermore, if the case is complex, it is good practice to involve a senior member of the Bar after explaining the reason why the client needs two counsel.

A. Immigration, Crime, and Family Law (cases involving children) and Vulnerable Clients (those with mental health issues and old clients)

Please take additional precautions when you undertake instructions from such clients. Where possible it is good practice to undertake instructions from such vulnerable clients via solicitors firms. Therefore, make sure that you are known to several solicitors firms dealing with such cases so that you could ask their help in case you have to refer a vulnerable client for them to take instructions and prepare the brief for you so that the client has adequate safeguards.

I have outlined the applicable rules of the Handbook of the BSB. Please check the rules in the BSB Handbook for further information.

It is prudent for all those who are in practice to familiarise themselves with the *Handbook of the Bar Standard Board*. Please make sure that you keep up to date with the amendments and the updated version of the Handbook.

Bar Standard Board has uploaded a Transparency Standards Guidance – Section 4 Checklists, and Supervision and Enforcement manual with a format (9 pages). In my view, it is good practice to download this manual and update the amendments where necessary and record the information as and when necessary.

In my view, there has been amendments to certain regulatory functions and rules so that regulatory functions have been taken over by the BSB e.g. Public Access registration – References to Public Access practitioners registering with Bar Council (Rules C120.1 and C121.1) have been amended to "the Bar Council (acting by the Bar Standards Board)". This reflects the fact that this is a regulatory function which is delegated to the BSB, but in practice undertaken by the Bar Council's Records Office.

In my view, the rules tend to overlap, and certain duties could be listed under the rule x, when the same duties or regulatory compliance could also be listed pursuant to x, y & z various other different rules, perhaps this is unavoidable. In short, there is overlapping rules and hence overlapping listing by the members of the profession.

1. Governance arrangements rule – rule C87.1
2. Risk management – **Rule C 89.5, Rule C 87.1 and CD6**
3. Data Breaches that you have reported to the Information Commissioner's Office Rules – C65, C66, C67, C68 & C69

If you are subject to any disciplinary or other regulatory or enforcement by another regulator, you are under a duty to make a Report – Rule C65

4. Instances of fraud, regulatory or near misses – Rule C87.1
5. If you are currently using or that you are planning to introduce, new and innovative technology – Rule C87.
6. Summarise other key risks that you have identified and describe how you manage and control such risks – Rule C87.1 and Rule C89.8
7. Are you planning any other significant changes to your practice within the next 12 months? – Rule C 87.1
8. What other information that you would like the BSB to be aware of in consideration of the risks associated with our respective practices? – Rule C87.1

Client Service and Delivery

9. Are we compliant with the price, service, and redress transparency rules? – Rules C103 and C159-169
10. What changes have you made in response to the new transparency rules and what (if any) impact you observed since these changes have been introduced? – Rules C103 and C159-169
11. Software that you use to manage your cases – Rule C87.1
12. If you receive instructions from other sources (apart from solicitors, licensed access instructions and public access instructions received directly from clients), you must make a record of such instructions and the sources of such instructions – Rule C79-85

Practice Management

13. How do you ensure, where applicable, the staff working with you are competent to do so? – Rule C87.1 and Rule C89.6
14. Does your practice have an up-to-date, documented Disaster Recovery Business Continuity Plan? – Rule C87.1
15. How do you monitor the changes in the BSB Handbook and make sure that you are up to date with regulatory requirements? – Core duty 10

Areas of Practice

16. The key controls that are in place for Public Access Instructions – oc30, oC31 & oC32

Training and Experience – Rules C120 and C121
You must be familiar with the procedure that you have for assessing the suitability of a client for Direct Public Access Work – Rules C122 and C123
Information provided to the lay client – Rules C125 and C127
Record keeping – Rules C128 and C129

Chapter 4
Supervision

The Bar Standard Board – Supervise barristers, chambers, BSB-regulated entities, and organisations that train pupils. They carry out impact and risk assessments. They check those that present risks to the Regulatory Objectives and to the public.

The BSB

i.   Monitor Continuing Professional Development (CPD) compliance;
ii. Issue Regulatory Returns to chambers and BSB-regulated entities;
iii. When necessary, visit those they regulate to help them to manage risks and to comply with the rules;
iv. Conducti reviews into areas of BSB regulations which pose threats to their Regulatory Objectives and where they think where and when they need to change the existing rules and;
v.   Consider a range of information that BSB receive about regulated individuals and chambers, BSB regulated entities to decide, when necessary, on the appropriate regulatory action to take in individual cases;

BSB Approach to Supervision – The aim is to foster a constructive relationship between the BSB and those they regulate. Efficiently run chambers and BSB-regulated entities operating at low risk are in everyone's best interest, resulting in less enforcement action and better protection and promotion of consumers' interests.

For further and detailed information, please refer to the Supervision Strategy and Guidance documents which are available from the Bar Standard Board.

Queries about Supervision – supervision@barstandardsboard.org.uk. The Supervision Team can also be contacted through the Bar Standards Board reception at 020 7611 1444.

I have settled a Draft Model for Sole Practitioners. This model can be amended to suit their individual requirements and can be used by those who are subject to supervision by the BSB.

Information to be included in the Model for Supervision based on the nature of the sole practitioner's practice.

Chambers............
Practising address...........
Telephone number...........
Fax number........................
Mobile number.......................
Email..................................
DX: ....

Barrister's name: ....

Barrister's year of Call............

Direct Public Access Course undertaken in the year ....

Litigation Practice Course undertaken in the year....

Areas of practice...............

Professional Development Courses undertaken within the last 12 months ......

1. Staff and other professional services assisting you in your practice

Name:

Their experience and qualifications:

Other service providers: Stationers such as Viking, PC world and service providers (list the service providers, stationers, etc.) to assist you with stationery, preparation of Trial Bundles and Appeal Bundles when necessary.

You must also inform your clients that you will be ultimately responsible for their cases.

Subscribe to legal websites, pay subscriptions, and obtain daily/weekly and monthly update on various areas of law. Also get help from various professionals on the website attending the seminars. Subscribe to various professional associations and obtain updates on current law. Provide opportunities for your staff to attend training courses when necessary. If possible, attend the seminars and professional development courses together with you so that you and your staff are familiar with the areas of your practice.

2. Receiving instructions

Ensure that you provide your clients with the Client Care Letter at the outset detailing your professional obligations to them. Ensure that they read it and understand prior to engaging you in their respective cases. Only if they agree with the proposed arrangement and agreement, ask them to sign the Client Care Letter to record their agreement to the terms of the engagement of your services. Inform them that you owe them a professional duty and that you are bound by the rules and regulations of the Bar Council. Please make sure that you undertake Due Diligence Test and that you ensure that the case is suitable for Direct Public Access and that the client is not suffering from any disability (dementia, mental illness, etc.) when instructing you.

3. Conference Venues

In addition to your chambers, make sure that you have facilities in place to arrange conferences in other venues. Arrange conferences in Rolls Buildings and other locations (Inns provide this facility as well) if there is Mediation or a Round Table conference with multiple parties. Those courts have venues for hire for conferences upon a payment of a fee. Furthermore, you can make arrangements to use facilities available in other chambers to hold conferences. Furthermore, you may book conference venues in other locations if necessary.

4. Due Diligence Test

Ensure that you undertake the Due Diligence Test initially before you take instructions. Ask for a certified copy of the passport, photocopies of any other identification documents such as driving licence, utility bills, etc. If the client is seeking advice on immigration matters, please check the source of funding the litigation to ensure the funds received are legitimate.

5. Instructions

It is prudent to advise your clients to give their instructions directly to you. If they give you instructions through third parties, please tell them that you will treat such instructions as information, until such time that your clients personally confirm their respective instructions to you. Inform them that in all your professional work, that you must follow the Bar Code of Conduct and the rules of Direct Public Access. Also inform them that you are covered by the Professional Indemnity Insurance and your practice complies with the Data Protection Act 2019 and other Regulatory Obligations of the BSB.

Inform them if you consider that a solicitor needs to be instructed in the best interest of the client or for some other professional reason that you will no longer be able to act for the client other than on the instructions of a solicitor. If you foresee that such a situation arising, give them notice well in advance so that they could make necessary arrangements.

6. Client contact

Make arrangements so that your clients can contact you at any time of the day. Provide them with your mobile number, landline number, and the phone numbers of your staff and the Practice Manager who is always aware of the nature of the case. Provide your email and phone numbers so that they can always contact you either by texts messages or via email or by correspondence addressed to you. Ensure the dates to comply with court directions are recorded in your mobile, office diary, counsel's notebook. Make sure Briefs (Civil or Criminal) are not returned to the client or solicitors at the last minute, also inform your clerk to enter the dates to comply with various directions and case listings in courts.

7. Proof of Identity and Money Laundering Regulations

Inform the clients that money laundering is a major concern and it is considered a serious criminal offence and that you have a duty to carry out money laundering checks to identify any potential offences and take necessary action. You have a duty to obtain satisfactory evidence of the identity of you clients. Therefore, make sure that they provide you with the following documents to verify their respective identities and addresses.

1. Certified copy of their current passports or full photocard driving licence as proof of their identities and;
2. Recent utility bills or bank/credit card statements, telephone bill or council tax which shows their names and addresses. The ID must be current, i.e. less than three months old.

It is essential that clients understand that these IDs are a strict requirement and that you will not proceed with their instructions without being satisfied about their respective identities.

8. What Has Been Agreed

Inform them in writing the nature of work that you will do for them and the timeframe for such work so that there are no misunderstandings between yourself and the clients. This may depend on the nature of the case and the circumstances.

9. Timescale

a. Please inform the clients about the time scale of the litigation. If it is a matrimonial case (which includes divorce, ancillary proceedings and contact with children if they are minors), evaluate the nature of disagreements between the parties and inform them not just the nature of the work but also the time scale. This may depend on the magnitude of the disputes, number of the parties involved and various other factors. Therefore, the time scale depends on the nature of the case and the type of litigation involved.

b. **Risks involved in litigation**

Inform the clients the nature of the risks involved. For example; If you undertake conveyancing – In a conveyancing transaction, unless there is an express agreement in place, any party may withdraw from the transaction, for instance, the purchaser may decide to withdraw from the transaction and as all pre-contractual work is subject to exchange, prior to exchange of contracts that the client (if your client is the seller) will have no cause of action in the absence of a signed agreement against the party who withdraws entitling your client to a cause of action. Such agreement must exist soon after the offer to purchase is accepted. Therefore, advise them that they must therefore satisfy themselves that the purchaser is genuinely interested in purchasing the property.

10. Costs

Advise your client's costs in litigation. There may be occasions that they would be ordered to pay costs of the opposite side even though may well have a good cause of action. Set out these costs' consequences in detail in your client care letter.

Please inform them that the costs orders need to be satisfactory otherwise the court may not allow them to proceed with the action. Also inform them if you think the matter should not go to the court for whatever reason, advise them the costs consequences.

11. Proof of source of monies to comply with Money Laundering Regulations

Inform your clients, that the rules require you to obtain proof of the source of their money (this may not be applicable in all transactions). For example, if it is from their own savings, you need to see copies of their bank statements or passbooks.

If monies are from the proceeds of a sale or a re-mortgage, then you may need confirmation of the proceeds from that transaction from the solicitors who acted for them. This requirement can be satisfied if they can produce a Completion Statement or a Financial Statement, which their solicitors would have given them during that transaction.

1. Inform the clients if they are obtaining monies from friends, relatives or private organisations, the rules require you to obtain proof of whom they are getting the money from, how much, and the nature of the agreement. In addition, if they are receiving money as a gift, you should ask them to produce the Deed of Gift signed by the person making the gift. Inform them that they must immediately inform you of any such arrangements so that you can ensure that you have all the necessary documentations in place so as to avoid any misunderstandings.

12. Fee Notes

Please set out the basis of how you charge for your work in the Client Care Letter. For example: hourly rate for the work. Also set out the Brief fee and fees for Refreshers where necessary. If the fees are agreed in advance, please set it out in the Client Care Letter and in the Fee Note. Please inform your clients that they are responsible for court fees and disbursements apart from your own fees.

It is good practice not to accept cash. In an emergency, you may accept cash if it is less than £500/–. But please issue a receipt for it contemporaneously or as soon as practicable.

13. Confidentiality

Inform your clients that you are under a professional and legal obligation to keep the affairs of your clients confidential. However, under recent legislation on money laundering and terrorist financing, that you are under a legal duty in certain circumstances to disclose information to the National Criminal

Intelligence Service. If you know or suspect that a transaction on behalf of a client involves money laundering, you are required to make a money laundering disclosure. If this happens, you may not be able to inform your clients that a disclosure has been made or of the reasons for it because the law prohibits 'tipping off'.

It is essential that your staff as well as your service providers e.g.: stationers, photocopying services and others dealing with your clients' information have a secure protection of your clients' data.

14. Capital Gains Tax

If there are Capital Gain Tax Liability or any income tax due to the HMRC, you must advise your clients to seek advice from an accountant.

15. Client Service/Complaints

If your clients have any complaints, queries, concerns, or suggestions for improvements about any aspect of the service that they have received, inform them in writing in your Client Care Letter that they should raise those issues directly with you.

1. Please send by post your Client Care Letter, the Fact Sheet, Privacy Policy and Cancellation Form to the client or hand it over to him or her in conference.

16. Storage of Files

Please inform your clients that at the end of their respective cases, you will store their files for a maximum of seven years, following which the files will be destroyed. If they require any documents from the file, then you ask them to inform you within 14 days of the conclusion of the case, following which the file would be sent for storage. If after this date, they require retrieval of the file for any purpose, then you reserve your right to charge an administration fee of ......

It is good practice to keep records of the cases for a longer period but please make sure that you comply with GDRP and The Data Protection Act 2018.

17. Storage of Data and Files

Please store the files in your laptop and have back-up copies in external devices. It is also good practice to contemporaneously log the items of work in your counsel's notebook under the heading of the case, and in your office diary. Please arrange the facility to store your work in a distance storage base organised by your internet provider. When the memory is full in your laptop, you could use the services of your service providers to store the data in a hard drive and store the hard drive and the old USB Sticks in the Secure Deposit Box either at your bank or some other secure place. Always comply with the GDRP.

18. Location of the files and cases

State what arrangements that you have in place to locate the files and cases, examples:

i.   Names of the clients and names of the parties involved in the case
ii.   Date, month, and year of instructions
iii.   The nature of the case (Matrimonial, Ancillary, Civil, Landlord and Tenant, Immigration, Probate, Crime, etc.)
iv.   Firm of solicitors instructed you
v.   If the cases are pursuant to Direct Public Instructions – the name of the client and when they gave instructions and when the case was concluded and outcome, etc.
vi.   Name of the Court where the Claim was issued and tried.

19. Termination of instructions

Please inform your clients the circumstances when they could terminate their instructions to you, and the way they could give you the notice of termination, for example, in writing to you at any time. Also inform them in your Client Care Letter that you reserve your right to charge a reasonable amount for any work already carried out and that your fees will not exceed the estimate of costs given. Furthermore, it is good practice to inform your clients that at any point if there is a conflict of interest arises, that you are required to stop acting for them, for example, in conveyancing matters, you expect to receive instructions from their respective lenders to act on their behalf. You may need to disclose information to the lenders that might be relevant to their decision whether to finance the transaction. If your clients tell you something that may affect your clients' ability to raise the mortgage or loan and that they do not want their respective lenders to know which might prejudice the lender's interest, you may have to stop acting both for your client and the lender.

20. Matrimonial or other Legal Disputes

In conveyancing transactions, if your clients are involved in divorce proceedings or any other legal disputes, advise them that they must disclose such infomration to you immediately prior to exchange of contracts.

21. Wills

Please advise your clients that in the circumstances, where their financial affairs are in the forefront of their mind, it would be appropriate to make a will or revise their existing wills so that the will considers their new circumstances. Even if you are not instructed in relation to drafting of the will or codicil, inform them of their right to do so if they wish and make a note of it.

22. Vulnerable Clients

You must have procedures in place to deal with vulnerable clients, identify vulnerable clients, their needs at an early stage and deal with them appropriately. Please ensure that you communicate effectively and positively to reassure them so that they can positively and effectively address the issues involved. If a client has any physical disability or other disability, please arrange a suitable venue to take instructions from him/her and inform the court in advance the facilities the client needs. In certain circumstances, when necessary, you should have arrangements in place to work with third parties who could assist the vulnerable clients so that they will achieve the best possible legal outcomes. If you have doubts about a client's mental capacity, you must obtain professional medical evidence to satisfy yourself that your client has the mental capacity to give you instructions.

23. Risks to the Barristers in Direct Public Access work.

In my opinion, please identify the risks to the legal practice generally. Thereafter your chambers specific problems as a Direct Public Access Barrister. In my view, it is a good way first to deal with the risks generally and then to deal with risks to your practice.

a. Barristers are now allowed to undertake Public Access work after attending and successfully completing the course, one year after they are qualified. Perhaps it may be the case that more time is needed to be adequately familiarised with the procedures. Some years ago, it used to be three years after full time-practice in an established set of Chambers but perhaps the time was reduced to one year because barristers in general found difficult to manage financially without public access work.

b. Most solicitors' firms have their own advocates and solicitors have the right of audience in all courts provided they satisfy the criteria. Therefore, traditional practice of solicitors retaining a barrister is no longer necessary.

c. Furthermore, legal aid is no longer available for most areas of work. Criminal legal aid has been continuously reduced over the years. Legal Aid Agency is unlikely to extend the legal aid to retain barristers for drafting pleadings and writing advice in criminal cases and opinions in civil cases. Traditionally this was the work of barristers.

d. New Internet Media (such as Twitter, Facebook, and websites) can have a disastrous effect in the circumstances where clients and the general public can make unjustified, unverified, unconfirmed comments on barristers (or for that matter any other professionals or individuals) without any proper basis. Law on Defamation and Libel is available but exercising this right through courts of law is an arduous and impracticable task due to the number of tweets and Facebook comments from all sorts of entities. Historically it was very often only a newspaper or a publication and much easy to identify the source of the publication and issue proceedings for defamation, Libel and/or Slander or even for an injunction. This may not always be the potential claim against social media.

e. Barristers are now allowed to practise in various organisations in different capacities. They can work in an organisation that has been authorised by an approved regulator to practise as a licensed organisation or a recognised organisation. These are organisations which are not directly controlled by the Bar Council. These organisations can be partnerships, companies, or sole principal, authorised to provide reserved legal services by an Approved Regulator other than the Bar Standards Board. Therefore, it is highly likely a barrister joining any such organisation has different rules to govern him in different capacities in these organisations.

f. Most chambers have been dissolved and they have merged with other chambers because they have fewer resources and unable to continue financially even with a relatively a small number of support staff. As they diversify their practice such as dealing with international clients, they need basic support resources.

24. Risks to Your Own Practice

Make a list of main risks in your practice and how do you deal with those risks so that you will minimise such anticipated risks.

a. Set it out chronologically your years of practice and experience since the call to the Bar. Identify your experience working with instructions from solicitors and working in chambers in all areas of work (identify the areas of your practice). Set it out when you established your Chambers as a sole practitioner. Identify the training and seminars attended at least within the last 12 months. Learn about the court structure geographically, where and when to file the documents and comply with directions.

b. Even though you may not have any more legal aid work, state how that you have sustained your practice on a relatively a small number of Direct Public Access clients. Identify your supporting staff and how they contribute to your practice. over the years and you deal with the administrative work. State your other support services, such as if you have an account opened an account with any of the Inns' Libraries or stationers to scan, copy and send documents when necessary.

c. If you have a professional website, make sure it complies with the Regulatory Requirements and that your website was created by a professional firm experience in providing such services. Please refer to the appropriate sections in the *Handbook of the Bar Standard Board.*

d. If you have an international practice, make sure that you inform the BMIF and the BSB. Make sure that you are familiar with the rules and practice in the international forum that you are practising so that your work will be governed by different codes of conduct, rules of different professional bodies and ensuring that there is no conflict of interest or damaging your clients' interest.

e. Deal with your volume of work and it may be relatively small due to the pandemic. Deal with your support services such as arranging a conference room away from your main Chambers (Most Direct Public Access Barristers work from home and have his or her home address as the main set of chambers). Make sure that you have arrangements elsewhere to accommodate a client using a wheelchair because you have to ensure that wheelchair access is compatible with Health and Safety Legislation.

f. It is a risk if you cannot pay your insurance premium to the BMIF and subscriptions and your other liabilities in time. Always try to arrange a reasonable overdraft and a reserve to deal with the unpredictable circumstances. Set out a business account to receive your income, with reference names of the clients and nature of the cases. This is necessary when preparing data for the BMIF and Inland Revenue so that you will not be late in presenting the necessary information to the proper authorities.

g. Install a CCTV system around your property (Chambers) and is connected via a security alarm system to a Professional Security Firm and the system is connected to your key holding company, your security firm, to the police, fire, and ambulance services so that your Chambers is safe and secure in the event of a burglary, fire, etc. This is important because you have all the court documents, clients' instructions, computers, laptops, books in your premises. Furthermore, please cover your old documents with a water-resistant material keep them safely from any accidental water damage in your property.

h. Make sure your computers have the passwords and professional antivirus protection to ensure that your clients' data are protected. It is good practice to arrange a business plan insurance (with monthly subscriptions) to request assistance any time of the day, month and year in case if you encounter problems with your computer software and the computer hard drive.

i. Make sure that you have a shredder to destroy private and confidential mail and other documents when necessary. Therefore, clients' data and privileged legal correspondence can be destroyed in the circumstances permitted by law. There, perhaps, is no need to engage a professional shredding company to destroy the privileged and unwanted documents. There are companies that you can engage to destroy documents at a reasonable cost. They give you a certificate as well to confirm that they have destroyed the documents safely. Do not place your privileged and client date in a bin. You must also ensure that your car is locked when you move around documents if you travel to work. Also make sure that your briefcase has a security lock so that no one could open it except you.

j. Make sure that there is someone in your chambers to receive post (signed post) and trial bundles, etc. when posted to your chambers and to have them logged. Always inform your clients to send the documents, signed, by post.

k. If you form the view that it is in your client's best interest to retain a senior member of the Bar or a Leading Counsel for your client on his instructions or on your advice, you could instruct him as an intervener, then it may be the case that you have to sign a different sort of client care letter that you instruct him or her and that you undertake to pay the other counsel's fee. Then it may be the case that you will have to open an Escrow Account (third party account) to receive your client's fees on behalf of the other counsel. In my view, the best practice is to ask your client to sign a client care letter with the other senior member of the Bar or the Leading Counsel and ask him to pay other senior member or the Leading Counsel's fees directly to him without you opening a third-party account. You must set it out in your Client Care Letter that you are not allowed to hold client's money on account in your chamber's business account.

l. Unpaid fees – Please set it out in your Client Care Letter how you would deal with unpaid fees.

    i. You could issue proceedings to recover your outstanding fees but see if it is cost effective because you would be spending time to recover unpaid fees at the cost of your valuable time working on your ongoing cases. It may be the case that it may not be cost effective to instruct a firm of solicitors or a debt recovery agency to recover your unpaid fees.

    ii. If a client is experiencing difficulties settling your fees, negotiate with the client and try if you could agree a different payment plan or reduced the fees by a certain percentage and accommodate him. In my opinion, do not allow the issues in relation to the fees to interfere with your professional obligations and duties when the case is continuing.

    iii. If client has a total disregard for your services and your claim for unpaid fees and does not want to pay your fees, you may have to make a judgement if it is viable option to sue him. This is a commercial decision to save additional costs and inconvenience.

Chapter 5
Data Protection Act 2018 and Compliance

PART 1 PRELIMINARY

1. 1.Overview
2. 2. Protection of personal data
3. 3. Terms relating to the processing of personal data

PART 2 GENERAL PROCESSING

1. Chapter 1. SCOPE AND DEFINATIONS

1. 4. Processing to which this part applies
2. 5. Definitions

2. Chapter 2. The GDPR

1. Meaning of certain terms used in the GDPR
    1. 6. Meaning of "controller"
    2. 7. Meaning of "public authority" and public interest etc.

2. Lawfulness of processing
    1. 8. Lawfulness of processing public interest, etc.
    2. 9. Child's consent in relation to information society services

3. Special categories of personal Data
    1. 10 Special categories of personal data etc. and criminal convictions etc. data

PART 3 LAW ENFORCEMNET PROCESSING

1. CHAPTER 1 SCOPE AND DEFINATIONS

2. Chapter 2 Principles

3. Chapter 3 Rights of the data subject

1. Overview and scope
   1. 43 Overview and scope

2. Information controller's general duties
   1. 44. Information controller General duties

3. Data subject's right of access
   1. 45. Right of access by the data subject

4. Data Subject's Rights to Rectification or Erasure Etc.
   1. 46. Right to rectification
   2. 47. Right to erasure or restriction of processing
   3. 48. Right under section 46 or 47 supplementary

5. Automated individual decision making
   1. 49. Right not to be subject to automated decision making
   2. 50. Automated decision making authorised by law safeguards

6. Supplementary
   1. 51. Exercise of rights through the commissioner
   2. 52. Form of provision of information, etc.
   3. 53. Manifestly unfounded or excessive requests by the data subject
   4. 54. Meaning of "applicable time period"

4. Chapter 4 Controller and processor

1. Overview and scope
   1. 55. Overview and scope

2. General obligations
   1. 56 General obligations of the controller
   2. 57. Data protection by design and default
   3. 58. Joint controllers

6. Chapter 6 Supplementary

Part 4 INTELLEGENCE SERVICES PROCESSING

1. Chapter 1 Scope and definitions

2. Chapter 2 Principles

3. Chapter 3 RIGHTS OF THE DATA SUBJECT

1. Overview
   1. 92 overviews

2. Rights
   1. 93 right of information
   2. 94 Right of access
   3. 95 Right of access supplementary
   4. 96 Right not to be subject to automated decision making
   5. 97 Right to intervene in automated decision making
   6. 98 Right to information about decision making
   7. 99 right to object to processing
   8. 100 Rights to rectification and erasure

4. CHAPTER 4 CONTROLLER AND PROCESSOR

1. Overview
   1. 101 overviews

2. General obligations
   1. 102. General obligations of the controller
   2. 103. Data protection by design
   3. 104 joint controllers
   4. 105 processors
   5. 106 processing under the authority of the controller or processor

3. Obligations relating to security
   1. 107 securities of processing

4. Obligations relating to personal data breaches
   1. 108 commutation of a personal data breach

7. 127 effects of codes issued under section 124 (4)
8. 128 Other codes of practice

5. Consensual audits
  1. 129 consensual audits

6. Records of national security certificates
  1. 130 Records of national security certificates

7. Information provided to the commissioner
  1. 131 Disclosures of information to the commissioner
  2. 132.Confidentality of information
  3. 133. Guidance about privileged communications

8. Fees
  1. 134 Fees for services
  2. 135. Manifestly unfounded or excessive requests by data subjects etc.
  3. 136. Guidance about Fees

9. Charges
  1. 137 Charges payable to the commissioner by controllers
  2. 138. Regulations under section 137 supplementary

10. Reports etc.
  1. 139 Reporting to parliament
  2. 140 Publications by the commissioner
  3. 141. Notices from the commissioner

PART 6 ENFORCEMENT

1. Information notices
  1. 142 Information Notices
  2. 143. Information notices restrictions
  3. 144. False statement made in response to information notices
  4. 145. Information orders

2. Assessment notices
    1. 146. Assessments notices
    2. 147. Assessment's noticers restrictions
    3. Information notices and assessment notices destruction of documents etc.
4. 148. Destroying or falsifying information and documents etc.

3. Enforcement notices
    1. 149 Enforcement notices
    2. 150. Enforcement notices supplementary
    3. 151. Enforcements notices rectification and erasure of personal data etc.
    4. 152. Enforcement notices restrictions
    5. 153. Enforcement notices cancellation and variation

4. Powers of entry and inspections
    1. 154. Power of entry and inspection

5. Penalties
    1. 155. Penalty notices
    2. 156. Penalty notices restrictions
    3. 157. Maximum amount of penalty
    4. 158. Fixed amount for non- Compliance with charges regulations
    5. 159. Amount of penalties supplementary

7. Guidance
    1. 160. Guidance about regularity action
    2. 161. Approval of first guidance about regularity action

8. Appeals etc.
    1. 162 Rights of appeal
    2. 163 Determination of appeals
    3. 164. Applications in respect of urgent notices

PART 7 SUPPLEMENTORY AND FINAL PROVISION

1. Regulations under this Act
   1. 182 Regulations and consultations

2. Changes of the data protection convention
   1. 183 Power to reflect changes to the data protection convention

3. Rights of the data subject
   1. 184 Prohibition of requirement to produce relevant records
   2. 185 Avoidance of certain contractual terms relating to health records
   3. 186. Data subject's right and other prohibitions and restrictions

4. Representation of Data subjects
   1. 187 Representation of Data subjects with their Authority
   2. 188 Representation of data subjects with their authority collective proceeding
   3. 189 Duty to review provision for representation
   4. 190 Post review powers to make provision about representation of data subjects.

5. Framework for data processing by Government
   1. 191 Framework for data processing by Government
   2. 192. Approval of the framework
   3. 193 Publications and review of the framework
   4. 194 Effect of the framework

6. Data sharing HMRC and reserve forces
   1. 195 Reserve forces data sharing by HMRC

7. Offences
   1. 196 Penalties for offences
   2. 197 Prosecution
   3. 198 Liability of directions etc.
   4. 199 Recordable Offenses

Schedules

Following passages were taken from a website.gov.uk

Data Protection Act 2018 Factsheet – Overview; what does the Act do? • Makes our data protection laws fit for the digital age when an ever-increasing amount of data is being processed. • Empowers people to take control of their data. • Supports UK businesses and organisations through this change. • Ensures that the UK is prepared for the future after we have left the EU. DCMS Secretary of State, Matt Hancock said: "The Data Protection Act gives people more control over their data, supports businesses in their use of data, and prepares Britain for Brexit. In the digital world, strong cyber security and data protection go hand in hand. The 2018 Act is a key component of our work to secure personal information online." How does the Act do it? • Provides a comprehensive and modern framework for data protection in the UK, with stronger sanctions for malpractice. • Sets new standards for protecting general data, in accordance with the GDPR, giving people more control over use of their data, and providing them with new rights to move or delete personal data. • Preserves existing tailored exemptions that have worked well in the Data

Protection Act 1998, ensuring that UK businesses and organisations can continue to support world-leading research, financial services, journalism, and legal services. • Provides a bespoke framework tailored to the needs of our criminal justice agencies and the intelligence services, to protect the rights of victims, witnesses and suspects while ensuring we can tackle the changing nature of the global threats the UK faces. Background The Data Protection Act 2018 achieved Royal Assent on 23 May 2018. It implements the government's manifesto commitment to update the UK's data protection laws. The Data Protection Act 1998 served us well and placed the UK at the front of global data protection standards. The 2018 Act modernises data protection laws in the UK to make them fit-for-purpose for our increasingly digital economy and society. As part of this the 2018 Act applies the EU's GDPR standards, preparing Britain for Brexit. By having strong data protection laws and appropriate safeguards, businesses will be able to operate across international borders. This ultimately underpins global trade and having unhindered data flows is essential to the UK in forging its own path as an ambitious trading partner. We have ensured that modern, innovative uses of data can continue while at the same time strengthening the control and protection individuals have over their data. The main elements of the 2018 Act are: General data processing • Implements GDPR standards across all general data processing. • Provides clarity on the definitions used in the GDPR in the UK context. • Ensures that sensitive health, social care and education data can continue to be processed while making sure that confidentiality in health and safeguarding situations is maintained. • Provides appropriate restrictions to rights to access and delete data to allow certain processing currently undertaken to continue where there is a strong public policy justification, including for national security purposes. • Sets the age from which parental consent is not needed to process data online at age 13, supported by a new age-appropriate design code enforced by the Information Commissioner. Law enforcement processing • Provides a bespoke regime for the processing of personal data by the police, prosecutors, and other criminal justice agencies for law enforcement purposes. • Allows the unhindered flow of data internationally whilst providing safeguards to protect personal data. Intelligence services processing • Ensures that the laws governing the processing of personal data by the intelligence services remain up-to-date and in-line with modernised international standards, including appropriate safeguards with which the intelligence community can continue to tackle existing, new and emerging national security threats.

Regulation and enforcement ● Enact additional powers for the Information Commissioner who will continue to regulate and enforce data protection laws. ● Allows the Commissioner to levy higher administrative fines on data controllers and processors for the most serious data breaches, up to £17m (€20m) or 4% of global turnover for the most serious breaches. ● Empowers the Commissioner to bring criminal proceedings against offences where a data controller or processor alters records with intent to prevent disclosure following a subject access request. Additional factsheets covering these measures are available from

https://www.gov.uk/government/collections/data-protection-act-2018

Key Questions and Answers ❖ How does the Act differ from the GDPR? The Act is a complete data protection system, so as well as governing general data covered by the GDPR, it covers all other general data, law enforcement data and national security data. Furthermore, the Act exercises a number of agreed modifications to the GDPR to make it work for the benefit of the UK in areas such as academic research, financial services and child protection. ❖ What is the impact on business? Organisations which already operate at the standard set by the Data Protection Act 1998 should be well placed to reach the new standards. The Act means that UK organisations are best placed to continue to exchange information with the EU and international community, which is fundamental to many businesses. The Information Commissioner has been working to help businesses to comply with the new Act from 25th May 2018 and is taking a fair and reasonable approach to enforcement after that date. ❖ Does the Act require organisations to improve cyber security? Effective data protection relies on organisations adequately protecting their IT systems from malicious interference. In implementing the GDPR standards, the Act requires organisations that handle personal data to evaluate the risks of processing such data and implement appropriate measures to mitigate those risks. For many organisations such measures include effective cyber security controls. Department for Digital, Culture, Media & Sport.

General Data Protection Regulation

There are 99 Articles listed in the General Data Protection Regulation ((EU) 2016/679) (GDPR)

I have set out below six key articles of the GDPR.

1. Rights of Individuals.
2. Right to Be Informed.
3. Right to Erasure ("Right to be Forgotten")
4. Data Protection Officer (DPO)
5. Obligations for Data Processors.
6. Data Protection Impact Assessment.

These articles provide EU citizens control over who can access, collect, process, handle, or share their "personal data." There are 11 Chapters dealing with the 99 Articles.

UK GDPR updated for Brexit

The EU General Data Protection Regulation "EU-GDPR", was established to protect the rights and freedoms of EU Citizens (Data Subjects), with respect to their Personal Identifiable Information (PII) and defined who and how their data could be used and retained by organisation around the world.

On 24th May 2018, one day before the "EU-GDPR" became law across the whole of Europe, the UK Government approved the updated Data Protection Act known as Data Protection Act 2018 (DPA 2018). DPA 2018, was a complete rework of the original 'Data Protection Act' of 1998 and incorporated into it, were all the clauses from the "EU-GDPR" and this legislation, therefore, became the basis upon which "Data Protection" would be judged within the United Kingdom.

As the result of Brexit and with effect from the 1st Jan 2021, the UK stopped being part of the EU and hence the "EU-GDPR" cease to protect the rights and freedoms of UK Citizens regarding their Personal Information. To prevent this becoming the case, the UK Government published an update to the DPA 2018 called the 'Data Protection, Privacy and Electronic Communication':-

Keeling Schedule – (As Amended By The Data Protection, Privacy And Electronic Communications (Amendments Etc) (Eu Exit) Regulations 2020 Laid On 14 October 2020).

To link with this "Data Protection, Privacy and Electronic Communication", the UK Government also revised the "EU-GDPR" to remove references to Europe and the EU and to refine it to the requirements of the UK. This document was published on the same data as the above communication and became the "UK-GDPR" document which shows with highlighting the changes made."

Chapter 6

Data Protection Act 2018

This is a comprehensive legislation dealing with various aspects of data collection, storage, disposal, etc. I shall only concentrate on the areas where sole practising members of the Bar should adhere in order to comply with the Data Protection Act 2018. I have set out below the main areas, but this list is not to be taken as an exhaustive list for compliance rules. Therefore, individual sole practitioners should investigate if they have to comply with any additional rules and regulations pursuant to the Act.

Overview and general duty of controller – see sections 34 to 40 of the Data Protection Act 2018.

The six data protection principles as follows:
Section 35(1) sets out the first data protection principle (requirement that processing be lawful and fair) – Legitimate grounds for collecting the personal data.

Section 36(1) sets out the second data protection principle (requirement that purposes of processing be specified, explicit and legitimate) – Limited for its purpose, Data should be collected for specified, explicit, and legitimate purposes.

Section 37 sets out the third data protection principle (requirement that personal data be adequate, relevant and not excessive) – Adequate, and necessary. The reason why the data is collected and for what legitimate purpose.

Section 38(1) sets out the fourth data protection principle (requirement that personal data be accurate and kept up to date) – Accuracy, Care should be taken to ensure that the data collected is accurate.

Section 39(1) sets out the fifth data protection principle (requirement that personal data be kept for no longer than is necessary) – Data should not be kept for longer than necessary and the data must be properly destroyed or deleted when it is no longer necessary.

Section 40 sets out the sixth data protection principle (requirement that personal data be processed in a secure manner) – Integrity and confidentiality, Data should be processed in a way that ensures appropriate security, including protection against unauthorised or unlawful processing, loss, damage, or destruction, and kept safe and secure.

See Section 3 of the Act for the relevant definitions in relation to the Terms relating to the processing of personal data

Personal data – means any information relating to an identified or identifiable living individual (subject to subsection (14) (c)).

Identifiable living individual means a living individual who can be identified, directly or indirectly, by reference to an identifier such as a name, an identification number, location data or an online identifier, or one or more factors specific to the physical, physiological, genetic, mental, economic, cultural or social identity of the individual.

Processing in relation to information, means an operation or set of operations which is performed on information, or on sets of information, such as:

a) collection, recording, organisation, structuring or storage;
b) adaptation or alteration;
c) retrieval, consultation, or use;
d) disclosure by transmission, dissemination or otherwise making available;
e) alignment or combination, or;
f) restriction, erasure, or destruction;

Data subject means the identified or identifiable living individual to whom personal data relates.

"Controller" and "processor", in relation to the processing of personal data to which Chapter 2 or 3 of Part 2, Part 3 or Part 4 applies, have the same meaning as in that Chapter or Part (see sections 5, 6, 32 and 83 and see also subsection (14)(d)).

Filing system means any structured set of personal data which is accessible according to specific criteria, whether held by automated means or manually and whether centralised, decentralised or dispersed on a functional or geographical basis.

The Commissioner means the Information Commissioner (see section 114).

As a sole practitioner, one must ensure that your staff, support organisations e.g.: stationers) trainees, students, voluntary staff, service providers and all those who work for you comply with the data protection policy and legislation.

Data in relation to an individual means, name, address, email address, phone number, fax number, DX number, date of birth, next of kin his or her CV current circumstances, financial information and this is not an exhaustive list.

Special Categories of Personal Data

Certain types of sensitive personal data are subject to additional protection under the GDPR. These are listed under Article 9 of the GDPR as "special categories" of personal data. The special categories are:

1. Personal data revealing racial or ethnic origin;
2. Political opinions;
3. Religious or philosophical beliefs;
4. Trade union membership;
5. Genetic data and biometric data processed for the purpose of uniquely identifying a natural person;
6. Data concerning health;
7. Data concerning a natural person's sex life or sexual orientation

Processing of these special categories is prohibited, except in limited circumstances set out in Article 9 of the GDPR.

Special category data is personal data that needs more protection because it is sensitive.

In order to lawfully process special category data, you must identify both a lawful basis under Article 6 of the UK GDPR and a separate condition for processing under Article 9. These do not have to be linked.

There are ten conditions for processing special category data in Article 9 of the UK GDPR.

Five of these require you to meet additional conditions and safeguards set out in UK law, in Schedule 1 of the DPA 2018.

You must determine your condition for processing special category data before you begin this processing under the UK GDPR, and you should document it.

In many cases you also need an 'appropriate policy document' in place in order to meet a UK Schedule 1 condition for processing in the DPA 2018.

You need to complete a data protection impact assessment (DPIA) for any type of processing which is likely to be high risk. You must, therefore, be aware of the risks of processing the special category data.

Checklist

1. Have you checked that the processing of special category data is necessary for the purpose you have identified and are you satisfied that there is no other reasonable and less intrusive way to achieve that purpose?
2. Have you identified an Article 6 lawful basis for the special category data?
3. Have you identified an appropriate Article 9 condition for processing the special category data?
4. Where required, have you also identified an appropriate DPA 2018 Schedule 1 condition?
5. Have you documented which special category of data that you are processing?
6. Where necessary, do you have an appropriate policy documents in place?
7. Have you considered whether you need to do a DPIA?
8. Do you include specific information about your processing of special category data in your privacy information for individuals?

9. If you use special category data for automated decision making (including profiling), have you checked that you comply with Article 22?
10. Have you considered whether the risks associated with your use of special category data affect your other obligations around data minimisation, security and appointing Data Protection Officers and representatives?

Summary

What is special category data?
What are the rules for special category data?
What are the conditions for processing special category data?
What are the substantial public interest conditions?

Special Category Data

The UK GDPR defines special category data as:
personal data revealing racial or ethnic origin;
personal data revealing political opinions;
personal data revealing religious or philosophical beliefs;
personal data revealing trade union membership;
genetic data;
biometric data (where used for identification purposes);
data concerning health;
data concerning a person's sex life and;
data concerning a person's sexual orientation

This does not include personal data about criminal allegations, proceedings or convictions, as separate rules apply. For further information, please see our separate guidance on criminal offence data.

Special category data includes personal data revealing or concerning the above types of data. Therefore, if you have inferred or guessed details about someone which fall into one of the above categories, this data may count as special category data. It depends on how certain that inference is, and whether you are deliberately drawing that inference.

What are the rules for special category data?

You must always ensure that your processing is generally lawful, fair and transparent and complies with all the other principles and requirements of the UK GDPR. To ensure that your processing is lawful, you need to identify an Article 6 basis for processing.

In addition, you can only process special category data if you can meet one of the specific conditions in Article 9 of the UK GDPR. You need to consider the purposes of your processing and identify which of these conditions are relevant.

Five of the conditions for processing are provided solely in Article 9 of the UK GDPR. The other five require authorisation or a basis in UK law, which means you need to meet additional conditions set out in the DPA 2018.

You must also identify whether you need an 'appropriate policy document' under the DPA 2018. There is a checklist and a template appropriate policy document shows the kind of information this should contain.

You must do a DPIA for any type of processing that is likely to be high risk. This means that you are more likely to need to do a DPIA for processing special category data. For further information, please see our guidance on DPIAs.

If you process special category data you must keep records, including documenting the categories of data. You may also need to consider how the risks associated with special category data affect your other obligations – in particular, obligations around data minimisation, security, transparency, DPOs and rights related to automated decision-making.

What are the conditions for processing special category data?

Article 9 GDPR lists the conditions for processing special category data:

a) Explicit consent;
b) Employment, social security and social protection (if authorised by law);
c) Vital interests;
d) Not-for-profit bodies;
e) Made public by the data subject;
f) Legal claims or judicial acts;
g) Reasons of substantial public interest (with a basis in law);
h) Health or social care (with a basis in law);
i) Public health (with a basis in law);
j) Archiving, research and statistics (with a basis in law);

If you are relying on conditions (b), (h), (i) or (j), you also need to meet the associated condition in UK law, set out in Part 1 of Schedule 1 of the DPA 2018.

If you are relying on the substantial public interest condition in Article 9(2)(g), you also need to meet one of 23 specific substantial public interest conditions set out in Part 2 of Schedule 1 of the DPA 2018.

What are the substantial public interest conditions?

The 23 conditions are set out in paragraphs 6 to 28 of Schedule 1 of the DPA 2018

Statutory and government purposes;

Administration of justice and parliamentary purposes;

Equality of opportunity or treatment;

Racial and ethnic diversity at senior levels;

Preventing or detecting unlawful acts;

Protecting the public;

Regulatory requirements;

Journalism, academia, art and literature;

Preventing fraud;

Suspicion of terrorist financing or money laundering;

Support for individuals with a particular disability or medical condition;

Counselling;

Safeguarding of children and individuals at risk;

Safeguarding of economic well-being of certain individuals;

Insurance;

Occupational pensions;

Political parties;

Elected representatives responding to requests;

Disclosure to elected representatives;

Informing elected representatives about prisoners;

Publication of legal judgments;

Anti-doping in sport;

Standards of behaviour in sport

You should identify which of these conditions appears to most closely reflect your purpose. Our detailed guidance gives you some further advice on how the conditions generally work, but you always need to refer to the detailed provisions of each condition in the legislation itself to make sure you can demonstrate it applies.

For some of these conditions, the substantial public interest element is built in. For others, you need to be able to demonstrate that your specific processing is "necessary for reasons of substantial public interest", on a case-by-case basis.

The public interest covers a wide range of values and principles relating to the public good, or what is in the best interests of society. It needs to be real and of substance. Given the inherent risks of special category data, it is not enough to make a vague or generic public interest argument. You should be able to make specific arguments about the concrete wider benefits of your processing.

For some of the conditions, you also need to justify why you cannot give individuals a choice and get explicit consent for your processing. In most cases, you must have an 'appropriate policy document' in place.

Rights of the data subject

General duties on the controller to make information available (see section 44).

confers a right of access by the data subject (see section 45).

confers rights on the data subject with respect to the rectification of personal data and the erasure of personal data or the restriction of its processing (see sections 46 to 48).

regulates automated decision-making (see sections 49 and 50).

makes supplementary provision (see sections 51 to 54).

This Chapter applies only in relation to the processing of personal data for a law enforcement purpose.

(3) But sections 44 to 48 do not apply in relation to the processing of relevant personal data in the course of a criminal investigation or criminal proceedings, including proceedings for the purpose of executing a criminal penalty.

(4) In subsection (3), "relevant personal data" means personal data contained in a judicial decision or in other documents relating to the investigation or proceedings which are created by or on behalf of a court or other judicial authority.

(5) In this Chapter, "the controller", in relation to a data subject, means the controller in relation to personal data relating to the data subject.

44 Information: Controller's General Duties

The controller must make available to data subjects the following information (whether by making the information generally available to the public or in any other way) —

   a) the identity and the contact details of the controller.
   b) where applicable, the contact details of the data protection officer (see sections 69 to 71).
   c) the purposes for which the controller processes personal data.
   d) the existence of the rights of data subjects to request from the controller—

   i.   access to personal data (see section 45).
   ii.   rectification of personal data (see section 46), and
   iii.   erasure of personal data or the restriction of its processing (see section 47).

   e) the existence of the right to lodge a complaint with the Commissioner and the contact details of the Commissioner.

(2) The controller must also, in specific cases for the purpose of enabling the exercise of a data subject's rights under this Part, give the data subject the following—

   a) information about the legal basis for the processing.
   b) information about the period for which the personal data will be stored or, where that is not possible, about the criteria used to determine that period.
   c) where applicable, information about the categories of recipients of the personal data (including recipients in third countries or international organisations).
   d) such further information as is necessary to enable the exercise of the data subject's rights under this Part.

(3) An example of where further information may be necessary as mentioned in subsection (2)(d) is where the personal data being processed was collected without the knowledge of the data subject.

(4) The controller may restrict, wholly or partly, the provision of information to the data subject under subsection (2) to the extent that and for so long as the restriction is, having regard to the fundamental rights and legitimate interests of the data subject, a necessary and proportionate measure to—

a) avoid obstructing an official or legal inquiry, investigation, or procedure;
b) avoid prejudicing the prevention, detection, investigation or prosecution of criminal offences or the execution of criminal penalties;
c) protect public security;
d) protect national security;
e) protect the rights and freedoms of others;

(5) Where the provision of information to a data subject under subsection (2) is restricted, wholly or partly, the controller must inform the data subject in writing without undue delay —

a) that the provision of information has been restricted;
b) of the reasons for the restriction;
c) of the data subject's right to make a request to the Commissioner under section 51;
d) of the data subject's right to lodge a complaint with the Commissioner, and;
e) of the data subject's right to apply to a court under section 167;

(6) Subsection (5)(a) and (b) do not apply to the extent that complying with them would undermine the purpose of the restriction.

(7) The controller must—

a) record the reasons for a decision to restrict (whether wholly or partly) the provision of information to a data subject under subsection (2), and;
b) if requested to do so by the Commissioner, make the record available to the Commissioner

45 Right of Access by the Data Subject

1) A data subject is entitled to obtain from the controller—

(a) confirmation as to whether personal data concerning him or her is being processed, and

(b) where that is the case, access to the personal data and the information set out in subsection (2).

(2) That information is—

(a) the purposes of and legal basis for the processing.

(b) the categories of personal data concerned.

(c) the recipients or categories of recipients to whom the personal data has been disclosed (including recipients or categories of recipients in third countries or international organisations).

(d) the period for which it is envisaged that the personal data will be stored or, where that is not possible, the criteria used to determine that period.

(e) the existence of the data subject's rights to request from the controller—

(i) rectification of personal data (see section 46), and

(ii) erasure of personal data or the restriction of its processing (see section 47);

(f) the existence of the data subject's right to lodge a complaint with the Commissioner and the contact details of the Commissioner.

(g) communication of the personal data undergoing processing and of any available information as to its origin.

(3) Where a data subject makes a request under subsection (1), the information to which the data subject is entitled must be provided in writing —

(a) without undue delay, and

(b) in any event, before the end of the applicable time period (as to which see section 54).

(4) The controller may restrict, wholly or partly, the rights conferred by subsection (1) to the extent that and for so long as the restriction is, having regard to the fundamental rights and legitimate interests of the data subject, a necessary and proportionate measure to—

(a) avoid obstructing an official or legal inquiry, investigation, or procedure.

(b) avoid prejudicing the prevention, detection, investigation or prosecution of criminal offences or the execution of criminal penalties.

(c) protect public security

(d) protect national security

(e) protect the rights and freedoms of others

(5) Where the rights of a data subject under subsection (1) are restricted, wholly, or partly, the controller must inform the data subject in writing without undue delay—

(a) that the rights of the data subject have been restricted,

(b) of the reasons for the restriction,

(c) of the data subject's right to make a request to the Commissioner under section 51,

(d) of the data subject's right to lodge a complaint with the Commissioner, and

(e) of the data subject's right to apply to a court under section 167.

(6) Subsection (5)(a) and (b) do not apply to the extent that the provision of the information would undermine the purpose of the restriction.

(7) The controller must—

(a) record the reasons for a decision to restrict (whether wholly or partly) the rights of a data subject under subsection (1), and

(b) if requested to do so by the Commissioner, make the record available to the Commissioner.

46 Right to rectification

1) The controller must, if so requested by a data subject, rectify without undue delay inaccurate personal data relating to the data subject.

2) Where personal data is inaccurate because it is incomplete, the controller must, if so requested by a data subject, complete it.

3) The duty under subsection (2) may, in appropriate cases, be fulfilled by the provision of a supplementary statement.

4) Where the controller would be required to rectify personal data under this section but the personal data must be maintained for the purposes of evidence, the controller must (instead of rectifying the personal data) restrict its processing.

47 Right to erasure or restriction of processing

1) The controller must erase personal data without undue delay where—

a) the processing of the personal data would infringe section 35, 36(1) to (3), 37, 38(1), 39(1), 40, 41 or 42, or
b) the controller has a legal obligation to erase the data.

2) Where the controller would be required to erase personal data under subsection (1) but the personal data must be maintained for the purposes of evidence, the controller must (instead of erasing the personal data) restrict its processing.
3) Where a data subject contests the accuracy of personal data (whether in making a request under this section or section 46 or in any other way), but it is not possible to ascertain whether it is accurate or not, the controller must restrict its processing.
4) A data subject may request the controller to erase personal data or to restrict its processing (but the duties of the controller under this section apply whether such a request is made).

DATA STORAGE

It is your responsibility to store the data securely. Data need to be stored as long as necessary to achieve the purpose for which the data was collected and also to comply with statuary obligations and to comply with your professional obligations such as to compile the information for your professional indemnity and to comply with the requirements of the Bar Standard Board.

It is good practice to encourage your staff to undertake data protection training.

I suggest that you set out steps that your chambers should implement to comply with the Data Protection Act 2018.

Step 1– Enrol yourself and your staff for a training program approved by the Bar Council.

Step 2 – Draft a Privacy Policy

Data Processed Register

Data Retention and Disposal Policy

Data Retention and Disposal Register

Data Security Policy

Data Protection Policy

IT Register

Third Party Data Sharing Register

Data Sharing Agreement – Controller to Controller

Data Sharing Agreement – Controller to Processor

Data Subjects Rights

Data Breaches Register

Crisis Management Plan

Chapter 7
Privacy Policy of The Chambers

Sole Practitioners' have a duty draft a Privacy Policy and you should include your name, practising address and your ICO number, its commencement, and its next renewal date.

Privacy Policy should include the following information:

1. Data controller's name and the registration number with the Information Commissioner's Office. Your practising address.
2. Data collection – The reason why you collect such data e.g.; to continue with your instructions and case.
3. The nature of the data that you collect including personal information:

Name, age, address, phone number, address, email address, national insurance number, passport number, bank details, next of kin's name and address if necessary, your history of education, training, employment details, information about your family where necessary, financial information, property, vehicles and other assets, criminal convictions if any and civil judgements recorded against you if any and any other court or tribunal findings against you such as bankruptcy.

There may also be circumstances, where it is necessary to collect special category of personal data such as racial or ethnic background, religious beliefs, genetic information, biometric data, data concerning health and sexual orientation

4. Lawful basis for processing your client's information:

i.   Obtain your client's consent (preferably in writing) before you collect the data.

ii.   Set out the reason. e.g. compliance with a legal requirement

iii.   For some legitimate reason,

iv.   to provide legal services.

v.   to comply with professional obligations

vi.   to report a threat to the public if there is any suspicious activities.

5. Special category data processing

You must get your client's consent preferably in writing. Such data may be necessary in furtherance of your client's litigation.

6. Criminal Data processing

This may be necessary in furtherance of criminal litigation, to get legal advice and to prosecute or to defend criminal proceedings.

7. Set out the reason why and how you use the information obtained from your client.

Examples: to provide legal advice and for other legal reasons.

8. Set out the reasons if you have to share your client's data with other third parties

Examples: to other lawyers involved in the case, to the court and to comply with legitimate Regulatory and the legal reasons.

9. Set it out if you share your client's data with third countries or International organisation and the reason why you must share the client's data with International organisations and other countries.

10. Set out your Data Retention and Disposal Policy

11. Set out the rights of your client.

Examples; he has a right to ask the reason why you need all such data and to instruct you to amend or delete his data and information, etc. in certain circumstances.

Please provide him with ICO's website:

http://ico/org.uk/for the public/personal information

Please also inform your client that he has a right to lodge a complaint if his data has been compromised and explain to your client that he has the right to make a request to you to obtain information as to the data that you have recorded.

Data Processed Register of ....Chambers

Address:

Telephone Number:

Email:

ICO Registration Number:

Policy commenced on:

Next review date:

Name of the Sole Practitioner:

The Register should include the following information:

1. **Categories of individuals:** Instructing Solicitors, Direct Public Access Clients, Employees, or any others such as Student or Pupil barristers.
2. **Categories of personal date:** Names, email addresses, any other personal data, bank details, etc. There may be other categories of personal data depending on the nature of the barrister's practice.
3. **Lawful basis for accumulating and processing the data:** Legitimate interest or contractual relations or any other depending on the lawful basis and the reasons you collected the data and the lawful basis for processing such data.

Legitimate interests for processing may include provision of providing legal services such as writing advice and/or opinion. Settling pleadings, communicating with other interested parties, and representing clients in courts and tribunals. This category includes criminal trials. This category may also include employees' CVs and the agreements made between you and the employees or may also include the basis upon how you train pupil barristers, etc.

Categories of special data may include medical records, medical reports, and personal information.

Lawful basis for processing special category of data may include in furtherance of court and tribunal cases. This may be necessary to establish claims and defence of clients. This may also be necessary for duties imposed by Health and Safety regulations. Categories may be based on individual circumstances.

You must also create a Template for Data Retention and Disposal Policy

As far as I am aware the GDPR does not state the period or time frame to keep personal data. The inference is that you could keep the data if you wish. It may be necessary that you have a valid reason to keep such data for a prolonged period depending on the nature of the information e.g. for future reference, historical purposes, or some other valid reason.

I do not see any problem if you use a fictitious name or identify the documents, the data and the information referring to a numerical number or a word from the alphabet. It may be the case that you want to preserve the pleadings that you drafted for future reference.

Please see for further information in the GDRP website and an update on corona virus and the GDRP

Data Retention and Disposal Register of ... ... Chambers

Address:

Telephone Number:

Email:

ICO Registration Number:

Policy commenced on:

Next review date:

Name of the Sole Practitioner:

The Register should include the following information:

Date when you received the data:

Date when you destroyed the data:

Chapter 8
Data Sharing Agreement – Model Template

I have set out here a model template Data Sharing Agreement. Please draft a Template with the information as set out herein with amendments where necessary to include your project. This may need further amendments based on the nature of the work to be undertaken by the parties. The model Agreement can be used with amendments where necessary depending on the nature of the project.

This agreement may not give rights to legal rights or actions to the parties involved. If the parties contemplate enforceable legal rights, they should have a Data Processing Agreement in place.

Please check if you need to undertake a Data Protection Impact Assessment (DPIA) where one is necessary. Please bear that in mind DPIA is mandatory requirement if you process personal data which is likely to expose a high risk to an individual's rights and freedoms.

Please refer for further guidance from your local Information Governance Team, Data Protection Officer (if you are a public body) or Caldicott Guardian.

This Data Sharing Agreement is made on (date)…. between
………….. List of Controllers (parties to the DSA)

1. Purpose, objectives of the information sharing: Set out here the reasons for sharing the data and your objective.
2. Controllers of the data: identify them individually

3. Processors: identify the respective processors and areas of their respective responsibilities and control, Identify the controllers to the whom the respective controllers should report.
4. Items of data to be processed – Identify the items in detail and the reasons for processing such data.
5. Check if there is a need for a DPIA
6. Article 6 GDPR – Personal Data – State precisely which article 6 condition applies

Legal Basis (One of the following must apply whenever you process personal data):

i. Consent: Set out clearly that you have your client's consent for you to process his or her personal data and for what purpose. Please make sure that your client has the capacity (age, etc.), he/she is of sound mind, and he or she is not suffering from impaired memory loss or dementia, etc.
ii. Contract: Processing of data is necessary for a contract which is intended to be made between you and the individual.
iii. Legal obligation: Processing is necessary to comply with Legislation and identify the legislation.
iv. Vital interests: Processing is necessary to protect life.
v. Public task: Processing is necessary to perform a task in the public interest or in your official duties and there is clear legal foundation.
vi. Legitimate interests: Processing is necessary for your legitimate interests or the legitimate interests of a third party, unless there is a good reason to protect the individual's personal data which overrides those legitimate interests. This does not apply if you are a public authority processing data to perform your official duties.

1. Article 9 GDPR conditions – Special Categories of Personal Data.

Article 9 GDPR prohibits processing of personal data revealing racial or ethnic origin, political opinions, religious or philosophical beliefs, or trade union membership, and the processing of genetic data, biometric data for the purpose of uniquely identifying a natural person, data concerning health or data concerning a natural person's sex life or sexual orientation unless the conditions set out in Article 9 is satisfied.

Examples of the conditions for processing special category data

i.   Explicit consent: The data subject has given explicit consent.

ii. Vital interests: To protect the vital interests of the data subject, who cannot give consent (life or death situations).

iii. Legal claims or judicial acts: To establishment, exercise or to defend of legal claims or whenever courts are acting in their judicial capacity.

iv. Reasons of substantial public interest (with a basis in law): This should be proportionate to the purpose.

v.   Health or social care (with a basis in law): Preventive or occupational medicine, for the assessment of the working capacity of an employee, medical diagnosis, provision of health or social care or treatment or the management of health or social care systems and services.

vi. Public health (with a basis in law): Protecting against serious internal or cross-border threats to health or ensuring high standards of quality and safety of health care and of medicinal products or medical devices.

vii. Archiving, research, and statistics (with a basis in law): Archiving purposes in the public interest, scientific or historical research purposes or statistical purposes.

viii. Other: State if you are processing data based on Schedule 1, Part 1, Data Protection Act 2018.

Note – UK GDPR and the Data Protection Act 2018 set out exemptions from some of the rights and obligations in some circumstances. Exemptions depend on the reasons for processing personal data. It you rely on an exemption you must justify your reasons.

2.   Individual rights and preferences: State how the individual rights and preferences are managed by the parties to this agreement. Individual rights are as follows:

Right to be informed, right of access, right to rectification, right to erasure, right to restrict processing, right to portability, right to object, and if applicable, rights in relation to automated decision-making profiling.

3. State how you will deal with any complaints in relation to the proposed data sharing:
4. Does the National Data opt-out apply to proposed purposes for data sharing? Y/N, if yes, please state how these would be dealt with.

In May 2018, National Data opt-out was introduced. Individuals can opt out of having their confidential patient information shared for reasons beyond their individual care, for example for research and planning.

5. Compliance with duty of confidentiality/right to privacy.

State how the procedures in place to comply with the duty of confidentiality. Consent, Statutory Gateway (e.g. approval under Section. 251 of the NHS Act 2006)

Statutory gateways refer to the statutes (Acts of Parliament) which expressly give statutory powers to certain public bodies to share information. Certain sections of those statutes provide for the sharing of information for specific purposes.

State if you are relying on statutory gateway and specify which and confirm whether it sets aside the common law duty of confidentiality. The NHS Act 2006 and the Regulations enable the common law duty of confidentiality to be temporarily lifted so that confidential patient information can be transferred to an applicant without the discloser being in breach of the common law duty of confidentiality. In practice, this means that the person responsible for the information (the data controller) can, if they wish, disclose the information to the applicant without being in breach of the common law duty of confidentiality. They must still comply with all other relevant legal obligations e.g. the Data Protection Act 1998. Approval also provides reassurance that that the person(s) receiving the information has undergone an independent review of their purposes and governance arrangements.

Note: I have set the above paragraph as an example. If there are situations similar to the above, it must be set out herein.

6. Is there any interference with Human Rights Act 1998 Article 8? Yes/No/Not applicable. If yes, state the reason why it is necessary to interfere with Human Rights and is it proportionate?

Article 8 protects right to respect for privacy and family life. It provides for the protection individual's right to private life, family life, home and correspondence which include letters, telephone calls and emails, etc.

7. Transparency. State how communications with the public will be undertaken. Examples Privacy notice, patient information leaflets/posters, information on website, etc.
8. How will the data sharing be carried out?

a. The mechanism by which the data will be shared and an explanation, why this is secure and which organisation is responsible for ensuring security of the data.
b. How any outputs/analysis will be shared and an explanation of why this is secure, necessary, and proportionate.
c. Frequency – including security precautions proportionate to the level of frequency.

Whether any information is being transferred outside the EU and, if so, relevant safeguards thus ensuring compliance with Article 45 of the GDPR.

Transfer of personal data to countries outside the European Economic Area may take place if these countries are deemed to ensure an adequate level of data protection. Third countries' level and standard of protection is assessed by the European Commission. Please check the list of the countries identified by the European Commission as having an adequate level of data protection where this is necessary.

9. Accuracy of the data being shared

State the procedure to ensure that data held and shared is accurate and how any updates will be shared with all recipients of the data.

10. Rectification of data that has been shared

State procedures in place for rectifying inaccurate data that has been shared and rectifying data that has been identified as inaccurate after sharing by the parties to the agreement.

11. Retention and disposal requirements of the information to be shared including details of the return of information to the source organisations (if applicable).
12. Management of data breaches

State the procedures in place for any breach of data security/confidentiality will be managed by the parties.

13. Specify any specific obligations on any party to this agreement.
14. Contacts – Information Governance and Caldicott Guardian

List here the IG contacts for each organisation.

Information: To share or not to share? Please refer to the Information Governance Review March 2013 for further information

A Caldicott Guardian is a senior person responsible for protecting the confidentiality of people's health and care information and making sure it is used properly. All NHS organisations and local authorities which provide social services must have a Caldicott Guardian.

Caldicott Principles which were updated in 2013, should be employed to examine the conditions under which patient-identifiable information is used or shared. Caldicot principles

I.   Justify the purpose for using confidential information
II.   Only use confidential information when it is absolutely necessary
III. Use the minimum information that is required
IV.   Access to confidential information should be on a strict need-to-know basis.
V.   Everyone must understand their responsibilities
VI.   Understand and comply with the applicable law

VII. The duty to share personal information can be as important as the duty to have regard for patient confidentiality

There should be a balance between the protection of patient information and the use and sharing of this information between agencies to improve care.

15. Commencement date of the Agreement.

Date the Agreement will come into force.

16. Review date of the Agreement

The date if, and when, and by whom (specify the job role) the agreement will be reviewed.

17. Review period – If applicable, state how long any review period will last.

18. Variation

State if the parties, or any party, can vary the terms of this agreement and if so, state how this is done.

19. Ending the agreement

State how a party ends the participation in the Agreement, and how data will be managed by the exiting party.

20. End date – State the end date of the Data Sharing Agreement.

Signature: Date:
Name:
Signature: Date:
Name:
Signatories to the Data Sharing Agreement

Chapter 9

Decided Cases, and Penalties Pursuant to the Data Protection Act 2018

This is not an exhaustive list of the cases. I have set out the following cases to show the complexity of the issues and how important it is to comply with the Data Protection Legislation to avoid penalties. This is an evolving area of law and there will be many more cases in the years to come. Almost all the countries in Europe takes data breached seriously and have issued severe penalties for various data breaches.

Medical Centre fined for abandoning sensitive information in empty building.

25 May 2018

Bayswater Medical Centre (BMC) in London has been fined £35,000 by the Information Commissioner's Office (ICO) after it left highly sensitive medical information in an empty building.

The personal data, which included medical records, prescriptions, and patient-identifiable medicine, was left unsecured in the building for more than 18 months.

In July 2015, BMC moved out of a former GP surgery but continued to use the premises for storage purposes.

In 2016, representatives of another GP surgery were allowed to visit the vacant building with a view to taking over the lease.

Once inside, they found unsecured medical records and other sensitive information and informed BMC, but the owners took no action to secure the data, despite repeated warnings by both the other surgery and the local Clinical Commissioning Group.

In February 2017, officers from NHS England visited the site and found a large quantity of extremely sensitive information left on desks, in unlocked cabinets and in bins. They ordered BMC to remove the information the next day.

Steve Eckersley, the ICO's Head of Enforcement, said

"Bayswater Medical Centre left their patients' most sensitive data abandoned and with no thought for the distress that this could cause them if it had been lost or misused."

The ICO ruled that:

BMC failed to secure the premises, or the data stored there, and allowed unsupervised access to the premises by others, who were not authorised to view the data;

BMC should have known that that exposing this highly sensitive personal information – and potentially losing it –would have caused substantial damage and distress; and

The contravention was heightened by BMC's failure to take prompt action to protect patient data for such a long time.

The ICO found that the severity of the breach merited a fine of £80,000, but this was reduced to £35,000 after BMC's ability to pay was taken into account.

Mr Eckersley said:

"It is our duty to stand up for people's data rights and to ensure that their sensitive personal information is protected.

"Out of sight is definitely not out of mind. We don't want anyone to think that they can avoid the law or their duties by abandoning personal data in empty buildings."

Notes to Editors

The Information Commissioner's Office upholds information rights in the public interest, promoting openness by public bodies and data privacy for individuals.

The ICO has specific responsibilities set out in the Data Protection Act 1998, the Freedom of Information Act 2000, Environmental Information Regulations 2004 and Privacy and Electronic Communications Regulations 2003.

The ICO can take action to change the behaviour of organisations and individuals that collect, use and keep personal information. This includes criminal prosecution, non-criminal enforcement and audit. The ICO has the power to impose a monetary penalty on a data controller of up to £500,000.

The European Union's General Data Protection Regulation (GDPR) is a new law which will apply in the UK from 25 May 2018. The Government has confirmed the UK's decision to leave the EU will not affect the commencement of the GDPR. The Government is introducing measures related to this and wider data protection reforms in a Data Protection Bill.

Anyone who processes personal information must comply with eight principles of the Data Protection Act, which make sure that personal information is:

fairly and lawfully processed,
processed for limited purposes,
adequate, relevant, and not excessive,
accurate and up to date,
not kept for longer than is necessary,
processed in line with your rights,
secure, and not transferred to other countries without adequate protection.

Civil Monetary Penalties (CMPs) are subject to a right of appeal to the (First-tier Tribunal) General Regulatory Chamber against the imposition of the monetary penalty and/or the amount of the penalty specified in the monetary penalty notice.

Any monetary penalty is paid into the Treasury's Consolidated Fund and is not kept by the Information Commissioner's Office (ICO).

To report a concern to the ICO telephone our helpline 0303 123 1113 or go to ico.org.uk/concerns.
website: https://ico.org.uk

Original article link: https://ico.org.uk/about-the-ico/news-and-events/news-and-blogs/2018/05/medical-centre-fined-for-abandoning-sensitive-information-in-empty-building/

GDPR penalties and fines

Now the Brexit transition period has ended, there are two versions of the GDPR (General Data Protection Regulation) that UK organisations might need to comply with:

The UK GDPR, which, with the DPA (Data Protection Act) 2018, applies to the processing of UK residents' personal data, and

The EU GDPR, which continues to apply to the processing of EU residents' personal data.

Learn more about the differences between the UK GDPR and EU GDPR

The UK GDPR and DPA 2018 set a maximum fine of £17.5 million or 4% of annual global turnover – whichever is greater – for infringements.

Th EU GDPR sets a maximum fine of €20 million (about £18 million) or 4% of annual global turnover – whichever is greater – for infringements.

However, not all GDPR infringements lead to data protection fines. Supervisory authorities such as the UK's ICO (Information Commissioner's Office) can take a range of other actions, including:

Issuing warnings and reprimands,

Imposing a temporary or permanent ban on data processing,

Ordering the rectification, restriction or erasure of data, and

Suspending data transfers to third countries.

London Pharmacy Fined After "Careless" Storage of Patient Data – 20 Dec. 2019

The Information Commissioner's Office (ICO) has fined a London-based pharmacy £275,000 for failing to ensure the security of special category data.

Doorstep Dispensaree Ltd, which supplies medicines to customers and care homes, left approximately 500,000 documents in unlocked containers at the back of its premises in Edgware. The documents included names, addresses, dates of birth, NHS numbers, medical information and prescriptions belonging to an unknown number of people.

Documents, some of which had not been appropriately protected against the elements and were therefore water damaged, were dated between June 2016 and June 2018. Failing to process data in a manner that ensures appropriate security against unauthorised or unlawful processing and accidental loss, destruction or damage is an infringement of the General Data Protection Regulation (GDPR).

The ICO launched its investigation into Doorstep Dispensaree after it was alerted to the insecurely stored documents by the Medicines and Healthcare Products Regulatory Agency, which was carrying out its own separate enquiry into the pharmacy.

Steve Eckersley, Director of Investigations at the ICO said:

110

"The careless way Doorstep Dispensaree sored special category data failed to protect it from accidental damage or loss. This falls short of what the law expects and it fall short of what people expect."

In setting the fine, the ICO only considered the contravention from 25 May 2018, when the GDPR came into effect.

Doorstep Dispensaree has also been issued an enforcement notice due to the significance of the contraventions and ordered to improve its data protection practices within three months. Failure to do so could result in further enforcement action.

Full details of the investigation can be found in the Monetary Penalty Notice here.

Notes to Editors

1. This is the first fine issued by the Information Commissioner's Office under the General Data Protection Regulation, which came into effect on 25 May 2018.
2. Special category data is personal data that needs more protection because it is sensitive. For example, health data, information about your sexuality, religion, or political beliefs.
3. The Information Commissioner's Office (ICO) is the UK's independent regulator for data protection and information rights law, upholding information rights in the public interest, promoting openness by public bodies and data privacy for individuals.
4. The ICO has specific responsibilities set out in the Data Protection Act 2018 (DPA2018), the General Data Protection Regulation (GDPR), the Freedom of Information Act 2000 (FOIA), Environmental Information Regulations 2004 (EIR), Privacy and Electronic Communications Regulations 2003 (PECR) and a further five Acts / Regulations.
5. The ICO can take action to change the behaviour of organisations and individuals that collect, use and keep personal information. This includes criminal prosecution, non-criminal enforcement and audit. For more information, see the Regulatory Action Policy.
6. To report a concern to the ICO telephone our helpline 0303 123 1113 or go to ico.org.uk/concerns.

Former GP Surgery secretary fined for reading medical records of 231 patients in two years – 29 November 2018

A former trainee secretary at a GP surgery has been fined after she admitted unlawfully reading the records of 231 patients in two years.

Hannah Pepper was employed at the Fakenham Medical Practice in Norfolk in August 2015 and her duties included lawfully accessing medical records to assist doctors, solicitors, and insurance companies.

However, despite being trained in the legal and ethical requirements for patient confidentiality, the surgery discovered in October 2017 that she had been reading a work colleague's patient file without consent.

A subsequent investigation by the surgery found that Pepper had illegally accessed 231 patient records with no valid reason. These included colleagues and their families, her own relatives, friends, and acquaintances and also members of the public.

In a subsequent interview with the Information Commissioner's Office (ICO) she accepted she had no justifiable reason for accessing the records and suggested that at times she struggled with the monotony of some of her tasks.

Pepper, aged 23, of Ashside, Syderstone, Norfolk, admitted four charges of unlawfully accessing personal data in breach of s55 of the Data Protection Act 1998 when she appeared at Kings Lynn Magistrates' Court.

She was fined £350 and was also ordered to pay costs of £643.75 and a victim surcharge of £35.

Mike Shaw, the ICO's Criminal Investigation Group Manager, said:

"People whose job allows them to access confidential and often sensitive information have been placed in a position of trust, and with that trust comes added responsibility. Data protection law exists for a reason and curiosity or boredom is no excuse for failing to respect people's legal right to privacy, just because you can do something, that does not mean you should."

If you need more information, please contact the ICO press office on 0303 123 9070, or visit the media section on their website.

Notes to Editors

1. The Information Commissioner's Office upholds information rights in the public interest, promoting openness by public bodies and data privacy for individuals.

2. The ICO has specific responsibilities set out in the Data Protection Act 2018, the General Data Protection Regulation, the Freedom of Information Act 2000, the Environmental Information Regulations 2004 and the Privacy and Electronic Communications Regulation 2003.
3. The ICO can take action to change the behaviour of organisations and individuals that collect, use and keep personal information. This includes criminal prosecution, non-criminal enforcement and audit.
4. A limited number of criminal enforcement cases – including this case – are still being dealt with under the provisions of s55 the Data Protection Act 1998 because of the time when the breach of the legislation occurred.
5. Criminal prosecution penalties are set by the courts and not by the ICO.
6. To report a concern to the ICO telephone our helpline 0303 123 1113 or go to ico.org.uk/concerns.

A new law came into force in the UK in May 2018, which outlines that employees can face prosecution for data protection breaches. As with previous legislation, the new law (the Data Protection Act 2018) contains provisions making certain disclosure of personal data a criminal offence.

A new law came into force in the UK in May 2018, which outlines that employees can face prosecution for data protection breaches. As with previous legislation, the new law (the Data Protection Act 2018) contains provisions making certain disclosure of personal data a criminal offence.

Google Fined by National French Data Protection Regulator.

On 21 January 2019, the French National Data Protection Commission (CNIL) has imposed a €50m (£44m) fine against Google LLC, following complaints made by the privacy rights groups None Of Your Business and La Quadrature du Net three days after the enactment of the General Data Protection Regulation (GDPR).

On 21 January, Google LLC (Google's French arm) was fined €50million by the Commission Nationale de l'information et des Liberties (CNIL) for various failings under GDPR.

The main failing CNIL found was that individuals using Google's services were not furnished with the requisite "fair processing information" (the information usually provided in privacy notices) by seemingly omitting to inform individuals about why Google processed their personal data how long their data was kept. The ruling also attacked the accessibility of the information saying that although most of the information was there, it was scattered around it site via various different "links". The second key failing was not meeting the GDPR standard of "consent" when providing personalised advert content. Under GDPR, consent must be sufficiently informed, specific, unambiguous, granular and be gained through a form of active acceptance. In the first instance the CNIL did not consider the consent to be informed enough as it ruled users were not given enough information about what giving their consent would mean in terms of the ad personalisation services Google would then push. The fine was also imposed in light of Google not ensuring that consent met the GDPR threshold through using pre-ticked boxes and not separating out consents for advert personalisation from other processing by Google.

The takeaways for your organisation are to ensure it's easy for your customers or service users to understand what you do with their data. Privacy notices should be clearly signposted and be as accurate as possible about what data is collected and why it is used. It also reminds us of the strict threshold consents must reach before they are valid. Businesses are certainly becoming savvier when it comes to making sure individuals are given consent for different purposes, but it's not uncommon to still come across the pre-ticked box! If your organisation relies on consent and would like Thorntons to review how you use it, please get in touch and we can give advice on whether you are meeting the GDPR standard.

Marriot International Suffer Unprecedented Data Breach

On October 30, 2020, the UK Information Commissioner's Office ("ICO") announced its fine of £18.4 (approximately $23.9 million) issued to Marriott International, Inc., ("Marriott") for violations of the EU General Data Protection Regulation ("GDPR"). This was a major *data breach* that may have affected up to 339 million guests.

In November 2018, Marriott reported a data breach that saw an estimated 339 million guest records exposed globally, of which around seven million related to UK residents. Marriott International announced that the personal data of 500 million of its customers had been compromised. The group, which operates hotel chains under the brands W Hotels, Sheraton, and Le Méridien among many others, said that they had reason to believe that certain of their computer systems had been hacked in 2014 which has now led to this breach. The number of people affected, which data relates to customer bookings from 2014 onwards, has now been revised and whilst they still cannot state the exact number, it believes the number of customer records now totals around 383 million. This remains an extremely large number of affected customers, and the hackers were able to access personal details, passport numbers, and in some cases payment information.

Although a breach of this scale is rare, there are various pointers that all organisations can take from this case. Firstly, it's a reminder to continuously monitor the technical and organisational security measures protecting personal data. Testing and monitoring of your organisation's security should be subject to regular review. Secondly, it's a reminder to have in place a practical guide for how to respond to a data breach. As well as having a clear process for how to report and assess breaches internally, your guide should be clear on what kind of breaches should be reported to the ICO, and perhaps statements to release to the media. Lastly, this case is a reminder of conducting regular audits of data held so that your organisation is always aware of how much data it actually holds. Marriott's reduced forecast of the number of data subjects affected is based on the fact they have now discovered that many of the accounts compromised actually relate to the same individual. If Marriott had an up-to-date list of active customers, it potentially could have been able to respond more quickly.

The ICO Acts Against Organisations for Failing to Pay the New Data Protection Fee

At the end of September, the ICO announced that it had begun formal enforcement action against organisations for failing to pay the new data protection fee. Since 25th May when GDPR came into force, organisations which are classified as data controllers have been required by the Data Protection (Charges and Information) Regulations 2018 to register with the ICO, and pay the applicable fee. Whilst the specific organisations have not been named, the ICO has confirmed they have issued 900 notices of intent to fine organisations which span "the public and private sector including the NHS, recruitment, finance, government and accounting". Of those 900, to-date 100 penalty notices have been issued which range from £400 to £4000, although the ICO has confirmed that the maximum could be £4350 depending on aggravating factors.

If you are unsure whether your organisation is required to pay a fee, please get in touch and we can advise accordingly.

The ICO Issued Its First Enforcement Notice for a Breach of GDPR

The ICO has issued its first formal notice under the GDPR to AggregateIQ Data Services Ltd ("AIQ"). AIQ, a Canadian company, was involved in targeting political advertising on social media to individuals whose information was supplied to them by various political parties and campaigns (such as Vote Leave, BeLeave, Veterans for Britain, and DUP Vote to Leave).

After an investigation by the ICO, AIQ was found not to have adequately complied with its obligations as a controller under the GDPR by: (1) not processing personal data in a way that the data subjects were aware of, (2) not processing personal data for purposes for which data subjects expected, (3) not having a lawful basis for processing, (4) not processing the personal data in a way in a way which was compatible with the reasons for which it was originally collected, and (5) not issuing the appropriate fair processing information to those individuals (commonly communicated through a privacy notice).

As well as those practical failings, the ICO also considered that it was likely that those individuals whose information was passed to AIQ and used for targeted advertising were likely to cause those individuals damage or distress through not being given the opportunity to understand how their personal information would be used.

The most interesting point about this case is that although the company is based in Canada, the ICO has still exercised its authority over those organisations which process data of those in the UK and ordered that AIQ must now erase all the personal data it holds on individuals in the UK. For a company which mainly deals in data and analytics, this could have a detrimental impact on its business operations in the UK. Although AIQ was passed the personal data from other organisations, this enforcement action demonstrates that it is still AIQ's responsibility to ensure that their use of the data was not incompatible with any of the purposes for which it was originally intended, and still incumbent on them to ensure individuals were aware of what they were doing with it. In addition, whilst there has been and continues to be a lot of emphasis in the media of the risk of large fines under GDPR, it is notable that no monetary penalty has been issued by the ICO, although the ICO has reserved its ability to do so should AIQ not comply with this notice.

Morrisons Held Liable for the Wrongful Acts of Its Rogue Employee by the Court of Appeal (England)

The circumstances of this interesting case centre around an employee whose rogue actions were still considered by the court to be attributable to the employer as a breach of the Data Protection Act 1998. The employee was employed by Morrisons Supermarkets as an internal IT auditor who in 2014, knowingly decided to copy the personal data of around 100,000 of Morrisons' employees onto a USB stick. At home, the employee then posted the personal data, which included names, addresses and bank details, onto the internet under the name of another Morrisons employee in an attempt to cover his tracks.

In finding that Morrisons was vicariously liable for the actions of the rogue employee, the Court concluded that there was a sufficiently close link between the employee's job role, and the wrongful action. That the wrongful event occurred outside the workplace was irrelevant, as the Court found that the employee in question was acting "within the field of activities assigned". Because the employee had access to the compromised personal data in the course of carrying out his role in facilitating payroll, he was specifically entrusted with that kind of information in order to do his job, so the Court decided that there was a sufficient link between the job role and the wrongful disclosure.

The key, striking, message from this case is that it is possible for employers to be held liable for rogue actions taken by its employees. Although this particular employee was obviously not acting within the expected confines of his job role, it is interesting that the Court still determined that employers may be liable for acts that it would normally reasonably consider out of its control. Although this incident occurred in 2014 and therefore decided under the Data Protection Act 1998, this case demonstrates how vital it is that organisations put in place appropriate technical and organisational security measures adequate for the type of data that is being held and also taking into account the risk of disgruntled employees and what they may do with their access to the information. This case also acts as a reminder of ensuring your staff are trained and aware of data protection and the role they personally can play in the protection of data, not just focusing on technical computer security which a lot of organisations pay more attention to. As remarked in this judgment, it also serves as a reminder of having adequate insurance in place in the event of a major data breach.

The ICO Receives Notification of Thousands of Breaches

Although organisations could report data breaches to the ICO under the Data Protection Act 1998, you will be aware that under GDPR there is mandatory reporting of breaches to the ICO in cases where there is a "risk to the rights and freedoms of individuals". The ICO has now reported that it has received notification of more than 8000 breaches in the 6 months since GDPR came into force. Last summer the ICO observed that many breaches that were being reported did not necessarily meet the threshold of risk, however they do welcome the honesty and transparency coming from organisations under legislation which is designed to strengthen rights for individuals.

With breaches requiring to be reported to the ICO within 72 hours of becoming aware, it is vital that mechanisms are in place internally for employees to understand how to report a breach and complete a risk assessment in the appropriate timeframe to assess whether it is reportable. If you would like any help compiling a data breach policy or risk assessment framework tailored to your organisation, please get in touch.

Chapter 10
Model Client Care Letter

Please amend it where necessary to comply with your practice. Emails addresses and the rules of the BSB Handbook set out here may change. Therefore, please update email addresses and guidance rules when, and where necessary.

………………....CHAMBERS

ADDRESS
TEL:
TEXT:
MOBILE:
DX
EMAIL:
Date:

PRIVATE AND CONFIDENTIAL
Name and address of the Client:
Your Ref:
Our Ref:
Dear …….

Re:……..

1. Thank you for your instructions in this matter. I confirm that I have received your instructions by email/letter/phone call on ……….. I would be pleased to accept instructions from you on the terms set out in this letter. Please read this letter carefully. It is important that you understand the terms and the basis upon which I accept your instructions to represent

you. If you agree with the proposed arrangement, please sign this letter to record your agreement. **I am authorised and regulated by the Bar Standards Board. In all my professional work, I must follow the Bar Code of Conduct and the rules of Direct Public Access. I am covered by the Professional Indemnity Insurance. I comply with the Data Protection Act 1998 & its subsequent amendments. I also comply with the Transparency Rules introduced by the Bar Council in July 2019**. I accept instructions from the Professional Clients (Solicitors) and other practising lawyers as well. Please refer to the Handbook of the **Bar Standard Board's (BSB) guidance for lay clients, which explains how the public access scheme works if you wish to obtain further information.**

2. **I am instructed by you pursuant to the Direct Access Scheme of the Bar.** There is no intermediary giving me instructions on your behalf. In carrying out the work under your instructions, I owe you a professional duty. If you are not known to me previously, I will ask you to prove your identity before I accept instructions from you. You must always give your instructions directly to me. If you give me instructions through other persons, I will treat such instructions as information, until such time that you personally confirm your instructions to me. I am a sole practitioner, and you can contact me directly either on my mobile number, landline or by email. Information and instructions given to me will be received in strict professional confidence. Only exception is that statutory and other legal requirements may cause me to disclose information which I have received, to governmental, and to other regulatory authorities without first obtaining your consent for such disclosure. English Law will govern the Contract we are making between us and any disputes will be subject to the jurisdiction of English Courts. If I am not available, you may contact my staff. ....Mr/Ms..................who assists me with clerical support and assistance. His/her mobile number is ....and his email is ....

3. I will act in your best interest. However, if I foresee a situation that you are unlikely to succeed and will end up paying litigation cost, I will

advise you. If you still wish to pursue this matter contrary to my advice, I will expect your instructions in writing before proceeding with this matter any further. In any event, if there are costs orders against you, you will be personally liable unless you have an insurance scheme to reimburse you for cost orders.

4. You will have to make your own arrangements regarding administrative services in connection with you case. My work on your instructions at this stage is to ....

Time Scale

The work I will carry out ....

I undertake to perform these services by .... (Depending on the nature of instructions

and work involved, I will set out the time scale and fee structure).

5. **Time Scale** is already agreed between us pursuant to the Directions of the Court and present circumstances. This again may need to be reviewed and revised if further Directions are forthcoming or factors beyond our control e.g.: In case the other party makes applications or due to additional Directions from the Court. I am unable to predict when your case will be concluded because this may depend on factors beyond our control such as availability of witnesses, other parties in your case and may also depend on the judicial time allocated to your case. Furthermore, you may have to bear in mind the possibility of prospective Appeals either by yourself or by the other parties involved in this litigation and additional time scale for such Appeals.

6. **The work I will carry out**

i.   The work you are instructing me to carry out is set out in my cover letter.

ii. If subsequent work is needed on this matter, and I am available to do the extra work, there will need to be another letter of agreement between us because I carry out all my work personally and cannot predict what other professional responsibilities I may have in the future, I cannot at this stage confirm that I will be able to accept instructions for all subsequent work that may be required by your case.

7. If I consider that a solicitor needs to be instructed in the best interest of you or for some other professional reason; I will no longer be able to act for you other than on the instructions of a solicitor. If I foresee that such situation arising, I will give you as much notice as possible.

8. If you would like to investigate the possibility of your financial means being such as to bring you within the scope of Public Funding (Legal Aid), you are advised to contact a solicitor who undertakes work on the basis of Public Funding. It is also important that you understand that I cannot do legal aid work unless I am instructed by a solicitor. Please let me know If you wish to discuss Legal Aid further before you instruct me.

9. I would be pleased to accept instructions from you on the terms set out in this letter and attachment. It is important that you understand my full terms as they will form a contract between us I thought it would be helpful to set out the work that I will carry out for you and the fees that I will charge for this work.

10. Fees

I have attached herewith a detailed fee structure for the anticipated work as agreed. However, this fee structure may need to be reviewed and revised if additional work is necessary and forthcoming in your case.

(Depending on the nature of instructions)

i. My fee for the advisory and drafting work described above will be a fixed fee of £........ /– for an hour. I am registered for VAT and my VAT registration number is........ /I am not registered for VAT. Therefore, my fees do not include VAT. You and I agree that I will not send you the work until you have paid my outstanding the fees.

ii. My fee for accepting the instructions to appear as an advocate on the occasion described above will be £.... (Brief Fee). You, and I agree that I will not attend the hearing unless you have paid the fee in advance. If for any reason the case takes longer than one day, I will charge an extra fee of £ ... per day (Refresher fee).

iii. I do not know how much work will be involved in your instructions. As a result, I cannot quote you a fixed fee at this stage. Therefore, I will charge you on a timely basis at £ ....../– hour. I will not carry out work that will cost you more than £ 750/– without your permission. When I have finished the paperwork, you have instructed me to draft, I will tell you how much the fee for the work undertaken. You and I agree that I will not send you the work until you have paid the outstanding fees.

11. Complaint Procedure

If you are dissatisfied with the services, you receive

If, for any reason, you are unhappy with the service you receive, my Chambers has a complaint procedure that you may follow. You have the right to complain against me if you are unhappy with my services. Please submit your complaint in writing. I will acknowledge your complaint forthwith and investigate it. I shall try to resolve the issues involved within 14 days. If you are still dissatisfied with the outcome, I will invite a member of the Bar from a different set of Chambers to investigate your complaint and see if the issues can be resolved. Further details about what to do if you have a complaint are set out in my terms. I am required to comply with the Code of Conduct in the BSB Handbook – details of where you can access the Handbook of the BSB are set out in my terms.

Please read this letter and the terms of our agreement carefully. If you are happy for me to take on this work and agree with my terms of agreement, please sign this Client Care Letter and the Attachment in the space provided and return the letter and the attachment to me. If you do not understand any of the terms, you should ask me to clarify and explain those terms.

12. Right to cancel

You have the right to cancel this contract within 14 days without giving any reason. The cancellation period will expire after 14 days from the day on which the contract is entered. To exercise the right to cancel, you must inform me of your decision to cancel this contract by a clear statement (e.g. a letter sent by post, fax or e-mail to the contact details provided on my letterhead). You may use the attached model cancellation form, but it is not obligatory. To meet the cancellation deadline, it is sufficient for you to send your communication concerning your exercise of the right to cancel before the cancellation period has expired.

Effects of cancellation

If you cancel this contract, I will reimburse you with all the payments received from you. I will make the reimbursement without undue delay, and not later than 14 days after the day on which I was informed about your decision to cancel this contract. I will make the reimbursement using the same means of payment as you used for the initial transaction, unless you have expressly agreed otherwise; in any event, you will not incur any fees as a result of the reimbursement. If you have requested me to begin the performance of services during the cancellation period, you shall pay me an amount which is in proportion to what has been performed until you have communicated to me your cancellation of this Agreement.

Client
Name;   **Signature:**   **Date:**
Counsel:
Name: **Signature**   **Date:**

Chapter 11
Attachment – Fact Sheet

My practice areas are as follows:

Set out the areas of your practice – Examples: Civil, Criminal, Immigration, etc.

The range of work I can carry out

Barristers advise on the law, draft documents for clients to use and appear on behalf of their client before courts or other organisations.

Here are some examples of work I can carry out.

1) I can draft letters on your behalf.
2) I can appear on your behalf to argue your case at court.
3) If a witness statement is needed from you, I can draft it from what you tell me. I may also be able to help finalise a witness statement from another person based on the information that person has provided.
4) There are circumstances, that you may need an Expert to give evidence on behalf of you. I can advise you on the need for expert evidence and on the choice of a suitable expert. Expert evidence is evidence about a professional, scientific, or technical matter provided by an individual with expertise in that area.
5) I can draft formal court documents for you. However, I cannot serve court documents on other parties or file them at court on your behalf. You will need to take responsibility for serving formal court documents on other parties and filing them at court. Serving court documents is the process by which papers relating to a case are put before the court or tribunal and the parties, e.g. individuals or organisations, involved in the case. This usually signals the start of formal proceedings.

6) I cannot go on the court record or provide my address to the court as the 'address for service' of documents (that is, the address which you are required to provide to the court for receipt by you of formal court documents sent by the court or other parties). You will be listed on the court record as a litigant in person. You will need to provide your own address as the 'address for service' of documents sent to you by the court and other parties.

As you are instructing me without a solicitor, you must be sure that:

1. you can do whatever is necessary for those matters that I cannot deal with; or
2. you have arranged with another person of suitable competence and experience to provide these services for you.

I am authorised by the Bar Council to litigate on behalf of my clients. If you instruct me to litigate, I am willing to accept your instructions but there is an additional fee for this service depending on the nature of the work. If you instruct me to litigate on your behalf, this need to be agreed between you and I.

I am the only person you are instructing to carry out the work in your case and I will personally do all the work agreed under this arrangement. I am a self-employed barrister. I have carefully considered your instructions and can confirm that I have sufficient experience & competence to undertake the work.

Circumstances when I may not be able to act for you and my availability

1. If for any reason I cannot carry out all the work you are instructing me to do, or if I want to suggest that another barrister (senior member of the Bar or a Leading Counsel (Queen's Counsel), instead of me, or as well as me to carry out the work for you, my clerk or I may propose this and explain why I have made this suggestion. However, another barrister will not carry out work for you unless and until you have agreed to instruct him or her and have also agreed to pay his fees. In such circumstances, you will be asked to sign a Client Care Letter with the

other member of the Bar, and you will have to pay his fees directly to him or her. I am not allowed to hold your money on account pay other members of the Bar or to pay disbursements on your behalf.

2. There may be times when my professional commitments clash. If I identify a possible clash of commitments and I am unable to work on your case, I will do my best to warn you as soon as possible and ask you how you would prefer to continue. As a result, it would be helpful if you would give me a telephone number on which I will always be able to contact you. In such circumstances, I may suggest the name of another barrister with a suitable level of seniority and expertise, who is willing to accept your case under the same terms as this agreement. You would then need to decide whether you want to instruct that barrister. I will also discuss with you the costs of retaining another barrister on your behalf. In such circumstances, you will be asked to sign a Client Care Letter with the other member of the Bar and you will have his fees directly to him.

3. As I carry out all my professional work personally, there may be times when I am not available to you. For example, if I am in court for a day or for several days in a row, I may be totally unavailable to all my clients during that time. If you are not able to contact me directly you can leave a message with my clerk or leave a message on my mobile/send me a text message or an email to me and I will respond to you as soon as possible.

i. As a barrister, I must follow the Code of Conduct in the BSB Handbook, which is available here:
https://www.barstandardsboard.org.uk/media/1553795/bsb_handbook

ii. That Code of Conduct requires me to consider whether a solicitor needs to be instructed in your best interest. If there comes a point at which I consider you need a solicitor I will no longer be able to act for you without the involvement of a solicitor. If I foresee that situation arising, I will give you as much notice as possible.

Legal Aid

It is possible that you may be eligible for public funding or "legal aid" as it is usually referred to. However, as a barrister I cannot do legal aid work unless I am instructed by a solicitor. If you want to talk to someone in more detail about getting legal aid, you should contact a solicitor who does legal aid work. They will be able to advise you about legal aid arrangements relating to civil cases e.g. where you are in dispute with another individual or organisation, and criminal cases e.g. where a crime may have been committed.

You can find out more information on the www.gov.uk website:

www.gov.uk/community-legal-advice

If you wish to be assessed for legal aid for a civil case, you can contact Community Legal Advice. This is a service which provides advice about family, debt, benefits, housing, education or employment problems. You can call them on: 0845 345 4345. You can also use their online legal aid calculator. This is a tool which allows you to check whether you can get legal aid for your case, if it is a civil case. This tool allows you to get online advice and can help you find a legal adviser near you:

legalaidcalculator.justice.gov.uk/calculators/eligiCalc?execution=e2s1

If you do not qualify for legal aid, you might like to consider whether you have any insurance policies that might cover your legal fees, or if the fees may be paid by someone else, for example a trade union.

I can advise and represent you if:

you make an informed decision not to seek public funding.

you make a public funding application, e.g. you have applied to get legal aid to help fund your case, that is rejected;

you do not wish to take up an offer of public funding (perhaps because you consider that the level of contribution you will be required to make is too much).

In signing these terms, you confirm that you have been informed that you may be eligible for public funding and where you can find further information. You are choosing to instruct me without the benefit of any public funding that may be available to you.

Fees

My fees for this work are set out in my cover letter.

Under these terms, you are responsible for paying the fees set out in my cover letter.

If you owe me any fees and do not pay them for more than three months after I give you a fee note, interest will be payable at 2% above the Barclays Bank base rate from 28 days of the date of the fee note.

Cancellation

Your right to cancel is set out in my cover letter.

You will lose the right to cancel this contract if the services have been fully performed at your express request within the cancellation period (in which case I will ask you to confirm that you understand you will lose your right to cancel).

Documents

You and I agree that:

1. I am entitled to keep copies of any documents you give me for my own professional records; and
2. I will return all your original documents to you when I have carried out the work you have instructed me to do.

I would prefer that you give me copies of documents (Indexed and paginated) rather than originals. However, if this is not possible, I may make a reasonable charge to you for producing photocopies.

General obligations

The information which you give me will be received in professional confidence. This means that I must maintain the confidentiality of any information you have shared with me and can only tell others about it if you give your consent for me to do so. The only exception is that statutory and other legal requirements may mean that I have to disclose (i.e. reveal) your information to governmental or other regulatory authorities, e.g. organisations, whose rules I must meet, without your consent and without telling you that I have made the disclosure. Statutory and legal requirements are rules or regulations that an individual must, by law, follow.

This contract will be governed by English law, and any dispute will be subject to the jurisdiction of the English courts. Jurisdiction means the power and authority of a court or tribunal to determine the outcome of a case and impose sanctions or penalties on those involved.

Barristers do not handle client money. Therefore, I am unbale to hold funds in my Chamber's Account on your behalf. However, I can advise and assist you to open an escrow account. This is in effect a third-party payment service.

Complaints

i. I hope you will be happy with the professional services I provide. However, if you are not satisfied, you should first refer the matter either to me or to my Chambers in line with my Chambers' complaints procedure. My Chambers' complaints procedure is included in the Client Care Letter.

ii. If you are not happy with my reply or my Chambers' reply, then you can contact the Legal Ombudsman. The Legal Ombudsman is a free, impartial and independent service set up by the Government which deals with complaints about the service you have received.

iii. You must complain to the Ombudsman within six months of receiving a final response to your complaint from myself or from my Chambers (provided the response specifically notifies you of your right to complain to the Ombudsman and of the six-month time limit). A complaint to the Ombudsman must also be made not more than six years after the act or omission complained about or not more than three years from the date when you should reasonably have known that there were grounds for complaint.

iv. For further details about how to make a complaint to the Legal Ombudsman, including guidance about the scheme rules. Please contact the Legal Ombudsman directly at:

Legal Ombudsman
PO Box 6806
Wolverhampton
WV1 9WJ
Email: enquiries@legalombudsman.org.uk (C101.2. b & c)
Phone: 0300 555 0333
Website: www.legalombudsman.org.uk

A guide to the scheme rules can be found on the Legal Ombudsman's website at:

http://www.legalombudsman.org.uk/downloads/documents/A-guide-to-our-revised-Scheme-Rules.pdf

Frequently Asked Questions concerning the new Legal Ombudsman can be found on the BSB's website: https://www.barstandardsboard.org.uk/complaints-and-professional-conduct/concerns-about-a-barrister

Client		
Name;	**Signature:**	**Date:**
Counsel:		
Name:	**Signature**	**Date:**

Cancellation Form

To [barrister's name, address, fax and email]:

I/We [*] herby give notice that I/We [*] cancel my/our [*] contract for the supply of the following services set out in the Client Care Letter dated……. [*]

Name and address of the client ………………,

Signature of client ………..

Date

[*] Delete as appropriate.

RECORD OF COMPLAINT

Name of the client:

Reference:

Date received:

Date of acknowledgement:

Date of detailed response:

Client's reply:

Further action proposed:

Subsequent action taken by the client

Resolution of the complaint and by whom?

Mediator:

Bar Standard Board:

Legal Ombudsman:
Method of resolution:

CLIENT'S SATISFACTION SURVEY

(To be completed after the conclusion of the case and/or instructions for any specific item of work as appropriate)

Name of the Client:
Reference:
Date received:
Satisfied: Yes/No
Partly Satisfied:
Dissatisfied:
Reasons:
Please state any suggestions for improvement:

Signed: Date:
Name:

Relevant Rules of the Handbook of the Bar Standard Board

Authorisation to practice – Rule CI03.1.
Time Scale to carry out the work – Rules C159.4 and C160

Fees – Rule C166, 2, 3 & 4
Complaint Procedure – Rule C101.2 a, b & c
The range of work to carry out – Rule C159.3

Chapter 12

As far as I am aware the Rules do not state that a Sole Practising Barrister should monitor Equality and diversity data. But I have set out the relevant information in case you wish to undertake recording the relevant data on a voluntary basis perhaps for your own records and reviews.

Equality and Diversity Policy of .... Chambers
Collection of information, use and destruction of the Data collected

1. I am a Sole Practitioner, and it is my professional duty to ensure that my Chambers, Name and address .... complies with the Bar Council Rules relating to Section 7 of the BSB Handbook and other Rules relating to Equality and Diversity.
2. It is my professional duty to adhere to all the Compliance Rules and Regulations of the Bar Council and I am duty bound to collect Equality and Diversity Data and publish an Anonymised Data Summary once every three years or make them available to the Bar Council in case they make a spot check or make the data available to members of the public in the event they ask for the Anonymised Data Summary. My chambers is committed to Equality and Diversity policy of the Bar Council. My Data Protection Register Reference is ....
3. I am the designated Diversity Data Officer in my Chambers. It is my duty to provide you with an opportunity to give information relating to equality and diversity. It is entirely a voluntary process. I have attached herewith the Equality and Diversity Questionnaire. You could complete the Questionnaire (if you wish) and return it to the Chamber's address or hand over the hard copy personally to me within 7 days.
4. This is an opportunity for you to submit information as to diversity to be published with anonymity. Please note that there is no mandatory

requirement for you to provide this information. It is a matter for you to provide this information voluntarily if you wish to do so.

5. All diversity date is securely kept, and I have security measures in place to protect your information. The reason why data is collected is to publish the data in an Anonymous Summary and to provide to the Bar Council (within three months) following the date of collection of the Data, to promote transparency concerning employment activities in the legal profession. I will not share your data with any other third party. The Anonymised Data Summary will be made available to the public at their request because there is at present no website for my Chambers. *(If you have a website, please refer to the rules in the BSB Handbook)*. In any event, Data relating to your sexual orientation and religion or belief will not be included in the anonymised summary format for publication.

6. I will ensure that the Equality and Diversity Data will be securely destroyed once the Data is anonymised and within 3 months after the date of collection of such data. The Questionnaire will be shredded. However Anonymised Data Summary will be kept for 12 months and would also be destroyed thereafter.

7. Please confirm by signing if you consent that I collect your Equality and Diversity Data and convert such Data to an Anonymised Summary Format to comply with the Equality and Diversity Policy of the Bar Council. You have a right to withdraw your consent and object to the use of your data by notifying me in writing and I will confirm in writing to you within three weeks that the steps have been taken to destroy your Equality and Diversity Data.

Sign: date:

Full name:

Equality and Diversity Monitoring Form

Please answer each question in turn by choosing one option only, unless otherwise indicated. If you do not wish to answer the question, please choose the option "Prefer not to say" rather than leaving the question blank.

1. About you

Which of the following categories best describes your relationship with Chambers?
Clerical staff providing casual clerking services
Any other
Prefer not to say

2. Age –

Please indicate your age in years.
Prefer not to say

3. Gender
a. What is your gender?

Male
Female
Prefer not to say

b. Is your gender the same as you were assigned at birth?

Yes
No
Prefer not to say

4. Disability

The Equality Act 2010 generally defines a disabled person as someone who has a mental or physical impairment that has a substantial and long-term adverse effect on the person's ability to carry out normal day-to-day activities.

a. Do you consider yourself to have a disability according to the definition in the Equality Act?

Yes
No
Prefer not to say

b. Are your day-to-day activities limited because of a health problem or disability has lasted, or is expected to last, at least 12 months?

Yes, limited a lot
Yes, limited a little
No
Prefer not to say

5. Ethnic group

What is your ethnic group?
Prefer not to say

6. Religion or belief

What is your religion, belief or any other?
Prefer not to say

7. Sexual Orientation

What is your sexual orientation?
Bisexual
Gay man
Gay woman/lesbian
Heterosexual/straight
Other
Prefer not to say

8. Socio-economic background

a. If you went to university (to study a BA, BSc course or higher), were you part of the first generation of your family to do so?

Yes
No
Did not attend university
Prefer not to say

b. Did you mainly attend a state or fee-paying school between the ages of 11 and 18?

UK State School
UK Independent/Fee – Paying School
Attended school outside the UK
Prefer not to say

9. Caring responsibilities

a. Are you a primary carer for a child or children under 18?

Yes
No
Prefer not to say

b. Do you look after or give any help or support to family members, friends, neighbours or others because of either:

Long term physical or mental ill-health/disability
Problems related to old age
No
Yes   How many hours
Prefer not to say

(Do not count anything you do as part of your paid employment)

Note – You can download an Equality and Diversity Monitoring Form to record the relevant data.

CPSIA information can be obtained
at www.ICGtesting.com
Printed in the USA
LVHW011212160622
721365LV00009B/248

9 781398 455030